Get It Right

A Guide to Strategic Quality Systems

Also available from ASQ Quality Press:

The Management System Auditor's Handbook
Joe Kausek

The Certified Quality Manager Handbook, Second Edition
Duke Okes and Russell T. Westcott, editors

The Quality Improvement Handbook
ASQ Quality Management Division and John E. Bauer, Grace L. Duffy,
Russell T. Westcott, editors

*Enterprise Process Mapping: Integrating Systems for Compliance
and Business Excellence*
Charles G. Cobb

*Unlocking the Power of Your QMS: Keys to Business
Performance Improvement*
John E. (Jack) West and Charles A. Cianfrani

*Development of FDA-Regulated Medical Products: Prescription
Drugs, Biologics, and Medical Devices*
Elaine Whitmore

*Design for Six Sigma As Strategic Experimentation: Planning, Designing,
and Building World-Class Products and Services*
H. E. Cook

*Developing New Services: Incorporating the Voice of the Customer
into Strategic Service Development*
Caroline Fisher and James Schutta

To request a complimentary catalog of ASQ Quality Press publications,
call 800-248-1946, or visit our Web site at http://qualitypress.asq.org.

Get It Right

A Guide to Strategic Quality Systems

Ken Imler

ASQ Quality Press
Milwaukee, Wisconsin

American Society for Quality, Quality Press, Milwaukee 53203
© 2006 by ASQ
All rights reserved. Published 2005
Printed in the United States of America

12 11 10 09 08 07 06 05   5 4 3 2 1

Library of Congress Cataloging-in-Publication Data

Imler, Ken, 1949–
 Get it right : a guide to strategic quality systems / Ken Imler.
  p. cm.
 Includes bibliographical references and index.
 ISBN-13: 978-0-87389-668-9 (soft cover, perfect bound : alk. paper)
 ISBN-10: 0-87389-668-8 (soft cover, perfect bound : alk. paper)
 1. Quality control. I. Title.

TS156.I45 2005
658.4'013—dc22   2005021046

ISBN-13: 978-0-87389-668-9
ISBN-10: 0-87389-668-8

Publisher: William A. Tony
Acquisitions Editor: Annemieke Hytinen
Project Editor: Paul O'Mara
Production Administrator: Randall Benson

ASQ Mission: The American Society for Quality advances individual, organizational, and community excellence worldwide through learning, quality improvement, and knowledge exchange.

Attention Bookstores, Wholesalers, Schools, and Corporations: ASQ Quality Press books, videotapes, audiotapes, and software are available at quantity discounts with bulk purchases for business, educational, or instructional use. For information, please contact ASQ Quality Press at 800-248-1946, or write to ASQ Quality Press, P.O. Box 3005, Milwaukee, WI 53201-3005.

To place orders or to request a free copy of the ASQ Quality Press Publications Catalog, including ASQ membership information, call 800-248-1946. Visit our Web site at www.asq.org or http://qualitypress.asq.org.

 Printed on acid-free paper

Quality Press
600 N. Plankinton Avenue
Milwaukee, Wisconsin 53203
Call toll free 800-248-1946
Fax 414-272-1734
www.asq.org
http://qualitypress.asq.org
http://standardsgroup.asq.org
E-mail: authors@asq.org

First and foremost, to my family: Gregory, whose skills as a copy editor helped make this book more readable; Brian, whose graphic design skills are displayed on the cover; and especially Margaret, my wife, best friend, and confidant—without her constant support the whole effort would never have happened.

This book is also dedicated to those courageous companies who have done an honest and critical introspective analysis and embarked on the journey toward strategic quality systems.

It is not enough to do your best . . . you must know what to do, and then do your best.

W. Edwards Deming

You must maintain unwavering faith that you can and will prevail in the end, regardless of the difficulties, and at the same time have the discipline to confront the most brutal facts of your reality, whatever they might be.

Jim Collins
Good to Great

Contents

List of Figures . . . . *xiii*

Foreword . . . . *xv*

Preface . . . . *xvii*

Chapter 1   Understanding Where You Are and Why . . . **1**
Perception Is Reality 4
Quality Is Not Completely Free 6
It's All About the Customers 9
Laying the Foundation 11
The Icing on the Cake 16

Chapter 2   The Evolution of Quality Systems **19**
The Gurus 19
Tools, Techniques, and You 22

Chapter 3   The Basics of the Approach **27**
Awareness and Understanding 30
Commitment and Communication 31
Direction and Dedication 32
Competency 32
Discipline 33
Risk-Based Analysis 35

Chapter 4   The Four Phases of Quality Systems **39**
Build Architecture and Connections   40
Evaluate and Align the System   74
Automate the System   79
Continuous Improvement   83

Chapter 5   Evaluating Your Quality Quotient **87**
Set Your Goals   89
Q^2 Is Cumulative   91
Management Responsibility Criteria   92
CAPA Criteria   94
Design Control Criteria   96
Change Management and Documentation Criteria   98
Internal Audit Criteria   99
Training Criteria   101
Production and Process Control Criteria   102
Purchasing and Material Control Criteria   104
Inspection and Testing Criteria   105
Calibration and Maintenance Criteria   107
Control of Nonconforming Product Criteria   108
Servicing and Installation Criteria   110
Statistical Techniques Criteria   111
Understanding Your Quality Quotient   112

Chapter 6   The Roles and Core Competencies in a
Strategic Quality System **115**
Executive Management   116
Functional/Departmental Management   119
The Management Representative   120
Quality Assurance and Quality Control   123
Purchasing and Materials   127
Design and Development   129
Other Functions   130

Chapter 7   The Role of the Consultant **133**
Run, Don't Walk   135
The Heart of the Matter   137

Chapter 8   Business Models and Quality Systems **141**
The Basic Models   141
Start-Ups   142
Turnarounds   145

Fast-Growth 148
The Silent Majority 150
Corporate Giants 152
World-Class Acts 155
A Brief Explanation of the Cost of Quality 157
The Constancy of Change 159

Chapter 9   Where Do You Go From Here? **161**
You've Got to Have Culture 161

Glossary *169*

Index *175*

List of Figures

Figure 1.1 Cost comparison. 11

Figure 1.2 Links between the four major systems. 13

Figure 3.1 Establishing and maintaining a strategic
quality system. 29

Figure 3.2 Risk-based analysis. 35

Figure 4.1 The four phases of quality systems. 41

Figure 4.2 Quality system elements. 43

Figure 4.3 Quality system architecture. 48

Figure 4.4 An integrated quality system. 49

Figure 4.5 Business risk table. 60

Figure 4.6 Simplified linkages in a quality system. 75

Figure 5.1 Quality quotient versus risk. 88

Figure 5.2 Quality quotient scorecard. 90

Figure 6.1 Management representative connections. 122

Figure 6.2 Quality system connections. 122

Figure 6.3 Quality system, quality assurance, and quality
control relationships. 123

Figure 8.1 The cost of quality reductions. 158

Figure 9.1 Establishing and maintaining a strategic
quality system. 164

Foreword

U
nfortunately, a crisis of some sort is frequently the precipitating event that causes a company to critically examine the manner in which it addresses the quality of the products it produces. One such crisis could be an enforcement action initiated by the Food and Drug Administration (FDA) such as an injunction—a devastating event that many companies do not survive. Another might be the performance failure of a commercially distributed product requiring a recall action and the resultant plaintiffs' suits. This, too, has been cause for collapse of businesses having an otherwise healthy prospectus. Stockholders, customers, employees, and, surprisingly, company management frequently ask, "How did this happen?" It is only then that questions begin to be asked about quality management.

This book provides a pragmatic and practical road map to the creation of a robust quality system—the antithesis of inelegant, defective, and possibly unsafe production. Ken Imler masterfully walks the reader through the whys and means to a quality system. His real-life experiences and examples allow even the most naïve reader an opportunity to understand the value of a quality system and how to establish one. Ken's approach doesn't focus on being in compliance with government rules, but rather highlights the broader benefits of a competent quality system. Improved economics derived from less waste, improved efficiency, enhanced customer satisfaction, and high employee morale are but a few of the benefits of a quality system. A strong quality system makes being in compliance a certainty.

Ken not only provides a road map to the creation of a documented quality system, he highlights the need to address organizational culture. The values and beliefs of an organization drive behaviors. A culture that is not aligned with quality principles and concepts can insidiously undermine the effectiveness of the most elegantly articulated quality system. Ken's use of hypothetical examples allows the reader to see clearly the impact management has in establishing organizational culture and the impact of culture on company behaviors.

This book is a straightforward, practical guide suitable for any company, large or small, that desires to preemptively avoid the nightmares caused by poor quality. From beginners to grizzled veterans, virtually all who have responsibility for quality products, whether in manufacturing, research and development, quality assurance, or (most importantly) management, can benefit from this book.

Ron Johnson
Executive Vice President
Quintiles Consulting
(former 30-year veteran of the Food and Drug Administration including director of compliance, Center for Medical Devices and Radiological Health, and regional director, Pacific Region)

Preface

As you open this book and start reading, the first question that may come to mind is, "How is this book any different from others?" This is a good question. It is one that I pondered for quite a while before I decided on the final content and construct of the book.

This book is based on over 30 years personal experience. It is meant to be the kind of book I wish I had at least 20 years ago before I: passed the ASQ Quality Auditor exam, became an ISO lead auditor, was a Crosby College graduate and trainer, became a Black Belt in Six Sigma, got an MBA, and attended over 50 courses and seminars on tools and techniques of quality and management.

I have written this book to be read and enjoyed by management-level quality and business professionals and the executives to whom they report. It has a strategic emphasis, and I feel the management overview distinguishes it from most quality assurance, quality control, and tactical references. It is aimed at key business stakeholders who are committed to a strategic quality system that will yield benefits beyond simply *having a quality system*. While my perspective is mainly from regulated industries, this book is designed to be applied by both regulated and nonregulated companies. For those companies in regulated industries, the strategies and techniques will drive beyond compliance and passed regulatory inspections and audits. For those in nonregulated industries, it will still provide a solid foundation and road map to success and increased profitability.

This book is intended to provide a unique but straightforward approach to business and regulatory requirements. It is intended for beginners looking for a road map and experienced professionals searching for effective ways to continuously improve quality systems.

HAVING A QUALITY SYSTEM IS NOT ENOUGH

Look at all of the companies that have quality systems and are having trouble. They are having trouble with the regulatory agencies that govern them and they are having trouble competing in their markets. *Why is this?*

Many companies just do not truly understand the difference between a simply having a quality system and the competitive advantage of a customer-centric strategic quality system that continuously drives value-added improvement. This book illustrates the difference and provides ways to get where you need to be.

A strategic quality system combines identifying and satisfying customer requirements with the tenacious application of continuous improvement tools and techniques to achieve the highest possible results and returns on investment.

The concepts in this book may not be revolutionary. They are, in fact, fairly intuitive and simple, built on common sense. The problem is that as the saying goes, "Common sense is not so common."[1] If it was, every company would be successful, and no company would have any problems identifying and satisfying their customers and regulatory agencies' requirements. Every company would be thriving, paying big dividends, and making profits for its shareholders. This, unfortunately, is not the case.

Also, common sense is not even enough; it only goes so far. A fundamental understanding of the concepts and approaches will only get you partway there. Looking at Walter Shewhart's original basics from the 1930s will only get you to a three-sigma level of quality. To be truly outstanding, you must move to six sigma or beyond by using unrelenting continuous improvement, as discussed in Chapters 4 and 9.

Many companies large and small fail to grasp the basic concepts involved with quality systems. Sure these companies have smart and dedicated people and experienced management; so why do they continue to have problems?

The answer, based on experience, is that management many times is not getting the right information from the quality system because the quality system is not set up to gather and analyze the right data. Another issue is that management is not willing to take a long, hard, honest, and sometimes painfully revealing introspective look at the organization, the quality system, and itself. Management in many organizations simply will not accept that things can be that bad. The company may be making significant profits but fail to understand that investment in a strategic quality system could increase these profits further. Companies fail to identify, early enough, that they are in an accelerating negative cycle that requires not just ever-increasing resources (capital and personnel), but a major change in how business is practiced day-to-day.

IT'S NOT ALL ABOUT POLICIES AND PROCEDURES

Quality systems, contrary to the belief of many companies, are not just about creating policies and procedures. Even though these policies and procedures are necessary for establishing and maintaining the quality system, the real prerequisite is a culture; a way of doing business. Until and unless this is truly understood and embraced by everyone in the organization, a truly strategic quality system culture cannot be established. Quality culture is an environment in which everyone is accountable for and responsible to the customers and their requirements.

Your company fits into one of three basic groups:

- Starting to create a quality system

- Revising a quality system

- Continuously improving a quality system

In this book I will tell you where and how to start strategically planning your quality system and provide ways to create, evaluate, and/or reengineer your existing quality system. The examples used are based on actual companies and experiences. They are not specific to any individual company, but are, rather, composites of the good and the not-so-good practices and approaches encountered over the years.

I invite you to take a journey of a few hours that took me years to realize. I have provided a road map that will make the journey a successful one. Here's your chance to get it right!

ENDNOTE

1. Thomas Paine, *Common Sense* (Philadelphia: 1776).

1

Understanding Where You Are and Why

sk yourself honestly, "Is my company really a winner or a me-too organization or a perpetual also-ran?" Does your company make money, but never quite get the brass ring? Does your company seem to have nagging problems that just don't go away? Things like customer complaints, field actions, nonconformances and deviations, recurrent rework and scrap—these all translate directly into wasted time, resources, and money. Additionally, they increase your risks.

Key metrics that define the health of your quality system and, therefore, your company include the number of field actions and how much (time, resources, lost opportunity, and money) you spend on them. Notice I did not say *invest* . . . you actually spend money here, *money that is lost and not recoverable.* The costs associated with your field actions are related to things like recalls, retrofixes in the field, nonscheduled preventive maintenance, repairs, and customer complaints. By just examining the volume and costs associated with these, one can pretty much understand the state of your business and quality system. More importantly, a field action indicates a lack of customer satisfaction, generally because of a failure to understand the customers and their requirements.

It is amazing that companies, many of which are actually fairly successful financially, spend up to or in excess of 25 percent of their annual operating budgets on these types of activities. This figure is based on actual calculations of the amount spent at several companies.[1]

In this book you will find some proven development, implementation, and continuous improvement keys that are part of a successful strategic quality system. Today's successful companies realize that it is all about the customers: knowing and understanding customers. Successful companies maximize value to the customer by providing the highest possible quality at the lowest possible cost. This sounds fundamental and easy, but be assured, if it were, everyone would be doing it. And doing it successfully. If your company accomplishes this, you will outcompete your competition.

Second place, third, or worse in a highly competitive market is most likely not going to make it today or in the future. Now this does not mean that there can only be one successful company in any given industry. What it does mean is that if your company is not prepared and does not have the advanced skills, you will not be able to compete successfully at the highest levels. Think of it in terms of professional sports. If you are playing in the minor leagues, do you have what it takes to get to the top professional levels and compete and win there?

You must also think in terms of *best-in-class*. You might be the best minor league team. If that is your goal, fine, you are best-in-class. If, however, your goal is to compete successfully at the top professional level, you have some significant challenges and work ahead of you.

Companies need to drive to be highly skilled and highly competitive. A strategic quality system creates both of these attributes, resulting in competitive advantage and high levels of customer confidence, satisfaction, and loyalty.

The first key to success is openly and honestly understanding and facing the facts. Sometimes these are brutal truths about what you can and cannot control. This means that you must identify the right key metrics, and gather and analyze the correct information. The second and equally important key is to understand that a strategic quality system is the basis of a self-fulfilling prophecy. If you set it up with the expectation that it will drive continuous improvement, and if you implement it correctly, it will!

A strategic quality system is not, contrary to popular belief, a collection of procedures, work instructions, and records. While these must be institutionalized, it is a culture and a way of doing business that is the heart of the quality system. That means your company, starting with executive management, must have an epiphany, one of those life-changing realizations, that continuing to do business as you have in the past and do in the present will doom you in the future. You cannot wish these into existence; you must invest time, money, and effort. But you should and must demand a reasonable return on that investment.

These policies, procedures, work instructions, and records are applicable even if your company is not in a regulated industry. The major difference between a regulated and a nonregulated arena is the amount of testing performed and the level of documentation and record keeping. Regulated industries are required to perform more testing and to create and maintain documentation that you might not do to the same level if unregulated. The business practices are basically the same. That is why it is important to use the perspective that strategically sound business practices will result in compliance in a regulated environment.

In reviewing the available texts and references, it is striking that they provide a plethora of insight as to what the quality system regulations and requirements are while failing to elaborate on a definitive strategic approach to the practical implementation of a quality system. Similarly, there are innumerable books and articles on quality tools and techniques that also fail to adequately bring all of the pieces together.

Too many companies fail to recognize that no matter the size, age, or organizational culture, a strategically planned, implemented, and maintained quality system adds value. In terms of the market, capitalization value for growing or large companies. The value can also be in terms of net present value to companies that are start-ups looking to be acquired by or form partnerships with other companies. A solid strategic quality system adds value to your business and makes it worth more. Companies that have a business strategy to develop technologies, sell the company or technology, and move on to the next company or technology can utilize quality systems to add value to the potential buyers. The inclusion and use of the quality system in these companies can actually make them more attractive to a potential buyer.

Strategic quality systems also identify, mitigate, and reduce business and regulatory risk, which can directly translate into bottom-line impact. Experience indicates that a solid quality system approach during due diligence is a good indication that the company has something other than just its intellectual property to offer. Start-up companies that have excellent people and/or product ideas are often devalued because the state of the quality system is such that it would require hundreds of thousands of dollars or more investment. This decreases the value of the rest of the assets and makes the company less attractive for acquisition or partnership. You can use the information in Chapter 5 on quality quotients when evaluating potential acquisitions. Some companies routinely use this type of evaluation as part of due diligence.

PERCEPTION IS REALITY

Examination of recent regulatory history shows that aggregate fines in the billions of dollars are being paid to the government's general accounting fund because of Food and Drug Administration actions against companies.[2] Businesses are similarly bleeding uncalculated dollars in lost opportunities and business practice inefficiencies.

Why is this the case? An argument can be made that companies do not willingly implement business practices that are not effective, efficient, or compliant with applicable regulations. Their perception is their reality, but their perception and, therefore, reality are flawed. They figure that because they have a quality system, things cannot be too bad . . . an *invalid perception*. They fail to face the brutal, but proven reality that this is not the case!

So how do companies end up paying and/or losing so much money? They do not strategically plan, implement, and maintain a quality system approach that identifies all of their customer requirements and utilizes risk-based decisions to drive investments. And how do all of these companies with their business professionals who have stellar education, experience, and credentials allow this to happen? They simply do not understand what a quality system is and how it impacts the entire company. This is not taught in most business programs. This lesson is most often learned through experience.

Similarly, companies are not performing adequate and robust business analyses regarding risk, exposure, and cost as part of the overall business equation. A company must be able to identify and quantify the risks and overall costs associated with these risks. A company must also be able to sort through the myriad of data and separate the significant few from the noise.

Most importantly, this information must be applied to prioritizing projects and activities and to allocating or reallocating resources. This is something that is not often done effectively. Companies think they are doing this, but in reality are not.

For example, one of many companies I have worked with was having trouble getting projects done on time, on budget, and effectively (20 percent of the projects are 80 percent done and 80 percent are only 20 percent done scenario). Management felt there were four major priorities: production, research and development, complaints, and customer satisfaction; with some 20 underlying projects. Surveying the employees showed that they were unclear about the four major priorities and that there were, in fact, over 200 priorities/projects going on throughout the organization!

The four priorities were actually far too ambiguous. Everyone in the organization felt the priorities and/or projects they were working on had been approved by management. Based on this, a new project was undertaken, using risk-based analysis, to evaluate all of the projects and see if the number could be reduced. The process resulted in the development of a tool that created quantitative measurements that could be used by management to truly prioritize projects and allocate resources. It resulted in the realization that the resources in the company were, in fact, overcommitted.

After consolidating chaos into discrete priorities and projects, management used the evaluation tool to identify the top 10 projects and prioritize them accordingly; aligning allocation of the company's resources. Interestingly, some projects were stopped. Management established and communicated the clearly quantifiable goals and the specific measurable performance metrics that were used to track the projects. Everyone knew precisely what the goals were, what the priorities were, and which priorities (and supporting projects), they were assigned to. If a new project or priority was identified, it was evaluated with the risk-based system. If it was a high priority, there could be two consequences; it could be the next project started, or it could bump an existing project. Until the company got additional resources, 10 was the limit to the number of projects/priorities that could be worked on simultaneously.

The results of this evaluation project were:

- Everyone in the company knew specifically what the priorities were and exactly how these priorities would be measured.

- Everyone in the company was assigned to specific projects/priorities with clearly specified and unambiguous costs, schedules, resources, and effectiveness metrics.

- Everyone's (including management's) performance and compensation (salaries, wages, bonuses) were linked to specific performance metrics (cost, schedule, resources, and effectiveness) for the projects/priorities on which they worked.

- Any new priorities/projects were evaluated and a limit of 10 was adhered to until the company capabilities and resources showed that it could successfully handle more.

The bottom line to all of this was that the company completed more projects on time, on budget, and more effectively. What's more, employee morale and involvement increased. This process required some additions and reengineering, using the concepts and tools described in this book, of key portions of the company's quality system.

Experience shows that companies large and small are all susceptible to the situations listed above. Companies are failing to recognize and take advantage of opportunities to reduce their business and regulatory risks. Many companies, including some very well known names, are not making the necessary investments required to reap the significant return available.

QUALITY IS NOT COMPLETELY FREE

Quality products and services require expenditures. There are certain fixed and variable costs that cannot and do not go away even with improved quality, cycle times, or throughputs. These are the costs of just being in business.

A short discussion for those of you who may not be familiar with Philip Crosby. One of his premises is that *quality is free*. In his book, *Quality Is Free*, he discusses the concept in terms of the cost of quality.[3] The cost of making products correctly the first time results in the lowest possible costs (the price of conformance to requirements). Doing things incorrectly adds costs (the price of non-conformance to requirements). He uses the idea that if you eliminate the price of nonconformance to requirements, then quality is free.

Also, quality improvement results do require investment and, at times, significant investment. Making the investments and reaping the returns can and should actually fund the quality system activities. If this is not the case, then you must determine why. Are you not making the correct investments? Or have you not identified the correct problems to address?

Too many companies are so focused on the short-term bottom line that they are blinded to the longer-term effects that some relatively modest investments can provide. Companies say that they "cannot afford to invest" or "now is not the right time." It is not a case of "can you afford to invest right now," it is a case of "can you afford *not* to invest and not to invest right now?" If you are not investing right now, the gap between you and the winning competitors is growing.

All good businesses should be willing to make an investment with a good return. I have personally seen returns well in excess of 50 to 75 percent in the first year. While this may not be typical, the reality is that a good quality system can actually pay for itself in cost, cycle time, and regulatory risk reductions.

Investing and being proactive are essential fundamentals in a strategic quality systems–based approach. Understanding what to do and implementing it are paramount. Converting to a quality systems approach is not rocket science. It also is not always easy. The larger the gap between where you are, in terms of culture, organization, and philosophy, and where you need to be, the larger the investment in time, money, and resources. Also, the larger the potential return.

A strategic quality systems approach is not a project and it is not a program. It requires champions and leaders, commitment and communication, dedication and discipline. It becomes a living and integral part of the company and, as such, must be nourished and maintained or it will wither and die.

Advocating that all companies should try to be world-class is not the goal of quality systems. Each company must understand its state of quality and capabilities. Your company may not have world-class capability, but you might be the best-in-class. In today's largely regulated world, a company must be at least state-of-the-art to have any hope of successfully competing. Think back to the professional baseball analogy. If you own a minor league team, you cannot successfully compete against a major league team. You might get lucky and win a game or two here and there, but you will not be successful in the long run. Companies must also realize that true world-class capability and performance is territory inhabited by only a few.

The process of establishing and implementing an effective and efficient quality system is not in opposition to the basics of good business. It actually creates proactive synergies that reduce both pre- and post-market costs, optimize process cycle times, and reduce exposure and risk.

An effective and efficient quality system cannot be driven solely by the intention to be compliant with applicable regulatory and statutory regulations and requirements. If you take this approach you will not be as effective, efficient, and profitable as you could be. Interestingly, you also will not be as compliant as you could be if you took the approach to develop and implement a quality system that is truly customer focused. A quality systems approach results in good business practices that are also compliant because you have understood and met all of your customers' requirements.

Surprisingly, many companies claim to be utilizing total quality management, Six Sigma, just-in-time and lean manufacturing, balanced score cards, and other quality tools and techniques.[4] And they are failing to integrate these with a strategic quality system approach to capitalize and leverage all available opportunities and solutions. A strategically applied quality system utilizes these tools and techniques on all business practices. Companies may be applying kaizen and poka yoke principles to developing and manufacturing products, however, they do not consistently look to routinely apply these same concepts strategically to the rest of the business practices.[5]

A very real question is, "How does this fit with customer satisfaction and focus on the customer?" A quality system approach is absolutely focused on customers. This includes identifying your customers, which means all of your customers both external and internal. It is predicated on establishing the customers' needs and requirements and then doing everything you can to not just satisfy them, but to delight them.

IT'S ALL ABOUT THE CUSTOMERS

A major area of concern and lack of understanding within companies is that they fail to recognize and treat regulatory agencies and bodies as customers. True, it is rare that a company provides its products or services to a regulatory agency, however, every company provides documentation and information regarding its products and services to regulatory agencies. Understanding this customer relationship with applicable regulatory agencies and bodies is critical to implementing a quality systems–based process.

Companies often implement what they call a quality system as a reactive step to a regulatory demand. These companies focus on the reactive correction of compliance issues and are often quite adept at making these changes. What they fail to recognize is that this is lost time and money.

A quality system approach must be an evolution, not a revolution. This process can be accelerated by strategic planning and investing. If you are a start-up, this can be proactive; the other business lifecycles require a certain amount of reactive remediation. This requires strategically planned analysis followed by a strategic implementation of the remediation plans. Your quality system should make processes simpler and easier, not more complex and prescriptive.

At this point, ask yourself some basic business questions:

1. Do you formally budget time, money, and resources for regulatory inspections and audits? If so, what percentage of your total annual operating budget is earmarked for this and why?

2. Do you formally budget time, money, and resources for responding to any adverse regulatory findings, product introduction delays, and related issues? Again, if so, how much and why?

3. If you don't budget for these possibilities, where do you find the time, money, and resources to react to these adverse regulatory findings? What opportunities do you forego to pay for these activities? What are you investing to proactively reduce and/or eliminate the need for these?

4. How much of your budget is targeted at identifying and understanding all your customers? Are regulatory agencies and internal customers considered?

Once you have considered these questions, you can start to understand your organization's tendencies. A good proactive approach invests with a demand for return on the investment. A reactive approach spends to fix problems. The reality is that most companies are a hybrid model. The utopia of a completely proactive approach is as elusive as finding the proverbial needle in a haystack. But do not stop searching!

If you annually budget time and resources for adverse regulatory consequences, then you are on the wrong track. If you are budgeting for these adverse events, take a step back and look at how you can better invest that time, money, and resources to proactively prevent these occurrences.

In Figure 1.1, the typical cost curve without a quality system shows the expenditures over the life of the product. It includes the premarket costs associated with design and development as well as the aftermarket costs required to keep the products and/or services operational. The cost curve utilizing a strategic approach shows what can happen with a strategically planned, implemented, and maintained quality system. The cost differences are based on investment in the premarket portion of the lifecycle of a product. It's the old adage of "pay me now or pay me later" and *later* is reactive and always costs more in the long run. These curves are based on actual experiences and are meant to provide a basic rule-of-thumb assessment of investment versus return. The curves may not be fully accurate for your particular company or industry, but the basic premise illustrated is applicable to all industries and many companies. The differences between the two curves are the result of a lack of a strategic quality system or an ineffective quality system. Specific issues will be identified and discussed in detail in Chapter 4.

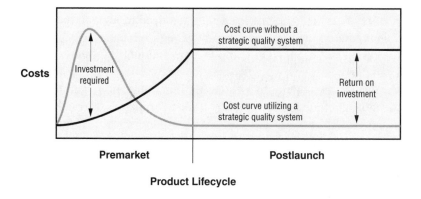

Figure 1.1 Cost comparison.

The required investment often appears to be stifling because it is a front-loaded investment, and the return is often not fully realized for several months. If you do not make the investment up front, you will waste money throughout the life of the product.

My experience has shown that the typical return on the investment is, at minimum, 25 percent over the first two years post market launch. Some situations have yielded returns as high as 400 percent over three years. The returns here are calculated as reduced costs in terms of:

- Reduced new product development cycle time

- Reduced new product development costs

- Reduced new product testing and clinical study costs

- Reduced post market launch costs

- Reduced service, warranty, and field corrective action costs

- Improved margins

LAYING THE FOUNDATION

There are four major portions that form the foundation, essentially driving the quality system and the business. These are derived from good business practices as well as regulations and statutory requirements. This begins to explain the need to include the applicable regulatory agencies in customers' requirements.

As an experienced and knowledgeable quality systems expert, I can fairly accurately predict the efficiency, effectiveness, and profitability of a company by evaluating this foundation. The four elements of the foundation are integral for a company's overall business practice effectiveness. They are all equal in terms of priority. If you lack one or one is weaker than the others, your quality system and business will be out of balance, causing increased cost, cycle times, and regulatory risk. Think of it in terms of quality *chi* and *feng shui;* energy, balance, and harmony.[6]

The four major systems include:

- Management responsibility

- Corrective and preventive action (CAPA)

- Change management

- Design control

As you will discover, these systems must be inexorably integrated to be successful and create the synergies necessary for effectiveness and efficiency. Figure 1.2 shows the relationships between these elements.

There must be well-established and maintained linkages within and between these elements. This helps ensure balance and consistency. This ties back to the strategic planning aspects of quality systems. How can you possibly hope to have a robust system if you have not strategically planned and prioritized the activities and resource allocations?

Design control is often thought of as not applicable to manufacturers. This is incorrect. Design control is still important even if you do not develop products. If you manufacture products that are developed somewhere else and transferred to your facilities, this is design control. If you manufacture with processes a third party develops and implements, these processes need to be transferred and validated, again as part of design control. If you make changes to products and processes, this is design control, and it becomes a case of how much design control you need to do or potentially redo;

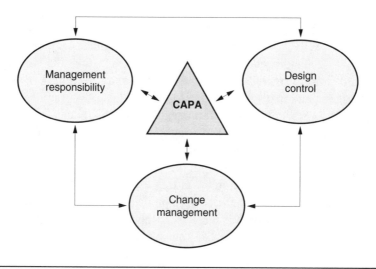

Figure 1.2 Links between the four major systems.

especially in terms of verification and validation of the changes. That is why there should be a hardwired link between design control and change control.

The important point to understand here is not just having these four major pieces in place. Think of it in terms of a puzzle; even if you have correct pieces, you still do not know what the picture is until and unless the pieces are assembled correctly. Or think of it in terms of your health. You must be in good physical, mental, and spiritual health to be ready for the continuous rigors of an active and productive life. If any aspect is not up to par with the others, your performance will suffer. Look back at the last time you sprained an ankle on a jog and the impact it had on your both your physical and mental state. Also think of the time it took to get back into both physical and mental shape. The same applies to your quality system. Being out of balance or having a setback in one area can impact the performance of the entire company.

In my experiences, I have not seen a single company with deficiencies in any of these key systems where cost, cycle time, and regulatory risk could not be significantly improved, provided the company was willing to accept the results of in-depth scrutiny and make the necessary investment and changes. Surprisingly, though, many companies plod along while incurring these additional costs and risks. Why? One of the major reasons is denial. Companies and company management are not willing or able to take the first step toward improvement. A comprehensive and absolutely honest, critical evaluation of the organization and its business practices must be done. Many companies don't want to do this because, "things are not that bad, we are still making profit and the regulatory agencies have not given us any real problems yet." Other companies are afraid of what they might find. An example is a good news/bad news scenario: The good news is that every product the company makes passes a comprehensive five-point inspection and functional test. The bad news is that there is 10 percent scrap, eight percent rework rate, and a three percent out-of-box failure rate in the customers' hands.

Companies are not willing to accept that the time-honored tradition of how the company has been run might, in fact, be flawed. They are similarly not willing to accept that significant change and investment might be involved to remediate the situation.

Another major issue is that company management is not aware of or integrated into the quality system. This is the "head is not connected to the body" syndrome. How can management make decisions regarding priorities and resource allocation if it has incomplete, flawed, or no data?

You might be thinking that this seems to be a business 101 book on business costs. To a certain extent you are correct. *The bottom line is, in fact, the bottom line.* Whether you call it profit, earnings before income taxes (EBIT), combined aggregate growth rate (CAGR), margin, or customer satisfaction, the key indicator of the effectiveness and efficiency of your quality system always translates back into money.[7] Cost, schedule, and regulatory risk can and should be translated into money. Money is the one key indicator that all management understands and reacts/responds to.

How much does your company currently invest in its quality system, and what is the rate of return on that investment? Don't look at spending any of your hard earned capital on the quality system. There is no return on spending other than the emotional goodwill you get. Don't take that cynically, emotional goodwill is a powerful tool and is part of the reward achieved from the implementation and maintenance of a solid quality system. Return on the investment, however, is the driver.

The rest of this book is dedicated to discussing and detailing the quality system approach, which will include analysis of symptoms and root causes, and providing strategic solutions for nonexistent, inefficient, and ineffective quality systems.

The purpose of this book is to provide a clear, concise, yet simple and compelling explanation of what quality systems are, how they integrate with customer requirements, and how they are really meant to be defined, documented, implemented, and maintained.

You will discover some basic concepts required to understand:

1. Where your company stands

2. What the gaps are

3. What to do about it

4. What the future prospects are for your quality system

Regulatory agencies and many associations clearly state the requirements and intent of their requirements. For example, the FDA has clearly stated recently that the intent of the regulations for drugs, biologics, and devices is a system-based approach that includes a foundation of risk management. This is becoming "industry standard" in many other industries as well. Those who do not identify and meet these regulatory and industry requirements are certain to incur greater long-run costs than those companies who proactively embrace this concept.

This brings up another point. Strategic quality systems are proactive while most other approaches are reactive. Many companies wait until they get into regulatory or business problems (in other words, increasing regulatory and/or business risk) before they react, only to find that they may have waited too long. Proactive organizations are better prepared to address issues while the risks are lower and, more importantly, to prevent the risks from increasing. This is not to say that proactive companies do not have issues, sometimes significant issues. It is to say that proactive companies are generally better prepared, organized, and capable of detecting issues earlier and reducing the risks faster and more cost-effectively. Proactive companies actively analyze risks and determine cost- and time-effective ways to mitigate or eliminate these risks.

The truth of the matter is that even without the specific regulatory, association, or industry practice requirements, a strategic quality system still makes good business sense. To see evidence of this, just look at the wide variety of industries that are now utilizing the tools and techniques previously described to run their businesses. Deming, Juran, and others have shown that the concepts and tools are applicable anywhere and everywhere. The Malcolm Baldrige National Quality Award (MBNQA) criteria use the same basic concepts of customer focus and have been utilized by a wide variety of companies over the years.[8] Be cautioned that the MBNQA is not for the faint of heart or the ill prepared. Your organization should be pretty mature and effective before considering applying for the MBNQA. The criteria, however, are an excellent place to look to see what *beyond state of the art* is.

THE ICING ON THE CAKE

The use of a strategic quality system approach will drive good business practices that in turn will be compliant with regulatory, association, and industry requirements, provided the correct requirements are identified and incorporated into the quality system. The basic business practices that result from a customer-centric and strategic quality system are the cake; meeting the requirements of your regulatory, association, or industry standards is the icing on the cake.

Key Takeaways

- Know where you are.

- Know where you want to be.

- Start learning and applying the basics.

ENDNOTES

1. This is based on actual calculations (ranging from 23% to 47%) of costs associated with recalls, corrections, rework, and scrap. It does not include lost opportunity costs. Companies include relatively small cap ($150 million) and large cap ($ multibillion) examples. The companies involved wished to remain anonymous.

2. *FDA Consumer Magazine* 1999 through 2004, *HHS News* 2000 through 2004.

3. Philip B. Crosby, *Quality Is Free* (New York: Signet, 1980).

4. Mary Walton, *The Deming Management Method* (New York: Perigee Books, 1986) and Mary Walton, *Total Quality Management and Business Excellence* (New York: Rutledge, Taylor & Francis Group, 2002); Thomas Pyzdek, *The Six Sigma Handbook: The Complete Guide for Greenbelts, Blackbelts, and Managers at All Levels, Revised and Expanded Edition,* 2nd rev. ed. (New York: McGraw-Hill, 2003); Hiroyuki Hirano, *JIT Implementation Manual: The Complete Guide to Just-in-Time Manufacturing* (New York: Productivity Press, 1998); John Allen, Charles Robinson, and David Stewart, eds., *Lean Manufacturing: A Plant Floor Guide* (Dearborn, MI: Society of Manufacturing Engineers, 2001); and Jessica Keyes, *Implementing the It Balanced Scorecard: Aligning It With Corporate Strategy* (New York: Auerbach Publications, 2005).

5. Anthony C. Laraia, Patricia E. Moody, and Robert W. Hall, *The Kaizen Blitz: Accelerating Breakthroughs in Productivity and Performance* (New York: Wiley Publishing, 1999); and Shigeo Shingo, *Zero Quality Control: Source Inspection and the Poka-Yoke System* (New York: Productivity Press, 1986).

6. Solala Towler, *Chi Energy of Harmony* (Toronto, Ontario: Andrews McMeel Publishing, 2003); Nancy Santopietro and Lin Yun, *Feng Shui: Harmony by Design* (New York: Perigee Books, 1996).

7. Joel G. Siegel, Marc H. Levine, Anique A. Qureshi, and Jae K. Shim, *GAAP 2005 Handbook of Policies and Procedures* (Gathersburg, MD: Aspen Law and Business, 2004).

8. Marion Mills Steeples, *The Corporate Guide to the Malcolm Baldrige National Quality Award: Proven Strategies for Building Quality into Your Organization (The Malcolm Baldrige National Quality Award Series)* (Burr Ridge, IL: Irwin Professional Publishing, 1992).

2

The Evolution of Quality Systems

A brief explanation of where the quality system concepts, tools, and requirements come from is often helpful in creating the required awareness and understanding necessary to strategically implement and maintain a quality system. If you do not understand the concepts, how can you plan the strategy? If you cannot plan, how can you successfully and effectively implement practical applications? You can't.

The current ideas and concepts were formally put together over 50 years ago and have been undergoing reformations and transformation ever since. The basic premises have been evolving over the years as new tools, techniques, and approaches have surfaced.

The early proponents of quality system concepts and tools include such people as Walter A. Shewhart, W. Edwards Deming, and Joseph M. Juran. Their initial ideas, tools, and techniques have been adopted and adapted by a myriad of others too numerous to list here. While I do not profess to be in the same league as these giants, I believe that by studying them, their history, and their approaches, I have been able to develop an approach that leverages and builds on their concepts and work.

THE GURUS

The basics of the whole approach go back to when Shewhart, who is generally considered the grandfather of total quality management, developed the Shewhart learning and improvement cycle. Shewhart was the first to really combine critical management thinking with tactical statistical analysis.[1]

The real groundswell of the quality systems–based approach—even though it was not labeled as such—started after World War II with Deming. His efforts to restart and reengineer the Japanese industrial infrastructure laid a good portion of the groundwork. Deming's applications of a total quality management (basic quality system) approach to statistical process control, effective process monitoring, and feedback put Japan on a path of development and improvement in manufacturing.[2] This would lead to the rise of a Japanese manufacturing machine that was far more effective in conquering the world than their war machine had ever been. By the 1960s "made in Japan" products were found in every industrialized country.

Curiously, the United States did not learn the lesson and take Japan seriously until the 1970s—after we had been beaten by the Japanese at the manufacturing game. Japanese manufacturing rose to become dominant and has been used as a model throughout the rest of the world. Kaoru Ishikawa's *fishbone* diagram—a proven root cause analysis tool—resulted in a robust mechanism able to ferret out the true root causes of process problems.[3] This root cause approach remains today as one of the most important concepts in process improvement for both business and manufacturing.

Joseph Juran, like Deming, spent considerable time in Japan after World War II. His approach to quality and the *Quality Control Handbook* added to the groundwork laid by Deming.[4] Juran's *Quality Planning Road Map* contains many of the basics of a quality system approach.

These, along with Genichi Taguchi's loss function, robust design using design of experiments, and Philip Crosby's zero defects and cost-of-quality approaches are only a few of the further adaptations of some of the basic concepts.[5] The more recent additions include *just-in-time manufacturing, lean manufacturing, balanced scorecards,* and *Six Sigma.*[6] These are all approaches that include basic quality system concepts and apply quality tools and techniques to identify and improve processes.

There are far too many tools and techniques available to discuss them all here. Let it be sufficient to say that a portion of the strategic planning process for a business is to investigate and evaluate the approaches, tools, and techniques and determine which are appropriate for that business, products, services, and culture.

Currently there are many technical and professional organizations, societies, and associations that have taken some of these tools and applied them to specific products and/or areas. A few of these include the International Electrotechnical Commission (IEC), the Institute for Electrical and Electronic Engineers (IEEE), the Association for the Advancement of Medical Instrumentation (AAMI), and the American National Standards Institute (ANSI).[7] As a side note, you should understand all of these in terms of requirements that apply to your products. Include these requirements when you start developing your quality system.

For example, if you design and manufacture products that contain electronics and software, then you need to be familiar with the requirements of the applicable IEC and IEEE standards. You should understand the myriad of information in the applicable international and domestic regulations, standards, and guidances applicable to your products and services. Remember to always identify and treat the agencies and organizations that develop and control this information as customers. I have limited the regulatory, association, and industry standards, regulations, and requirements to the FDA-regulated industries.

Aerospace and automotive companies have been practicing basic quality system approaches for many years. There are many other industries that also use the basics of the quality system approach, but they are too numerous to identify here. Each of these industries also has an extensive list that applies.

There may not be regulatory consideration in every industry. There may be literally hundreds of associations and industry standards that may be applicable to your products. You must have expertise in your organization to ferret these out, understand them, and include them in your strategy.

More examples include the Global Harmonization Task Force (GHTF), a group of international subgroups and technical committees founded by the European Union, the United States, Canada, Australia, and Japan working to generate guidances that will bridge the various medical device requirements and regulations.[8] Similarly, on the pharmaceutical side, the International Conference on Harmonization (ICH) has established a series of quality, safety, efficacy, and multidisciplinary topics that provide guidance to companies.[9]

There are two major reasons why these standards, guidances, and regulations are brought up. The first is that they are required if you want to market your products, so directly or indirectly the organizations and regulatory agencies that institute these standards and guidances need to be recognized and included as your customers. They have specific user needs that must be met. Secondly, all of the organizations and agencies have developed these standards, guidances, and requirements based on customer requirements, which is the basis for the quality system.

The most successful and competitive companies are making significant investments in creating capabilities and core competencies in tools and techniques such as Six Sigma, quality function deployment, lean manufacturing, statistical process control, and balanced scorecards, to name just a few. Significant capital investments are also being made in the areas of computerized systems and specialized information technology (IT) applications and solutions. These are all potentially synergy creating, provided they are value-added parts of a well thought-out strategic plan.

TOOLS, TECHNIQUES, AND YOU

Do you need all of these tools and techniques to implement a quality system approach? The answer, surprising to some, is *no*. But this is definitely a qualified, not an absolute answer.

The qualified answer recognizes that conscientious evaluation and utilization of these tools, techniques, automated processes, and IT solutions can significantly reduce your quality system implementation time, but they are not absolutely mandatory. The key concept here is to strategically plan your processes and then look to automate them. Do not start with automation and try to make your processes fit the automation. Start with creating functional and user requirements before looking at solutions in automation and IT. Without the strategic thinking from both a business and a quality system perspective, these investments will not yield the highest possible levels of return. They may actually be a drain of resources and capital that could have been better invested in other areas to maximize the return on the investment. I have seen companies spend literally millions of dollars on IT solutions that failed because:

- User and functional requirements were not established as the first step.

- The solution was not tailored to the needs.

- The system was forced to match the IT solution.

Automation and IT solutions are areas where many companies go astray. For example, consider Unique Products Inc. (a fictitious company). The quality and purchasing managers independently decided they each needed a database management system for all of the data they collected and used. They each went to a different person in the IT group with a request for a database management system. The quality manager had heard of a system that a friend at another company used, so he requested that package. The purchasing manager left it to the discretion of the IT person, because they were the experts. Within a couple of weeks, two separate suppliers were showing their database management systems to quality and purchasing, respectively and independently. A few months later, the installations were complete and the two systems were up and running. So far so good?

The quality manager was now looking at comparing internal and external problems regarding incoming quality. Data from both databases needed to be collated and analyzed. The problem was that the two databases had different formats, were on different servers, and could not talk to each other. The solution was to have an in-house IT person create customized applications to take information from both databases and merge it into one. This required special customized inquiries to be written, which would work only with the custom database and not with either of the purchased databases.

Can you see where we are headed here? If the true user and functional requirements had been established for all affected or potentially affected customers (purchasing, quality, management, and possibly others), a better single solution could have been developed rather than having the three systems that Unique Products ended up with. The initial and maintenance costs would have been much less, and the system efficiency would have been much greater.

Creating or hiring core competencies in the use of these tools, techniques, and IT solutions can require significant capital and resources. This is why it is important to first perform the honest and comprehensive analysis to identify the gaps and the risks associated with those gaps. You can then look at the quality system implementation investment options and determine what level of investment makes sense.

Now focus on the impact of all of these quality system tools and techniques on your company's need for an effective and efficient quality system. Many regulatory agencies are utilizing this risk-based approach and are adopting the quality system concepts in their regulations. The important concept here is that over the years, regulated companies have come to the realization that the regulations and requirements make good business sense. This is why companies must recognize these regulatory agencies as customers. Understand their requirements, meet them, and wherever possible, exceed their expectations.

Imagine the cost savings if you don't get a lengthy list of issues from your regulatory agencies, delaying the introduction of new products and services. Ask the companies that have regulatory issues how much better off they would have been investing a fraction of the reactive capital and personnel costs proactively in infrastructure, training, and systems development. How much could you save if your interactions with regulatory agencies went smoothly and effectively?

The point of this explanation of the evolution of the quality system is to stress that the regulatory agencies governing your company *must* be included in your consideration of customers. Remember, it is all about the customers. If you miss or fail to understand any of these customers and underestimate their requirements and potential impact, the consequences are that your quality system and strategy will be incomplete and, therefore, unsuccessful. These consequences can be dire and definitely will lead to added risk that may, in turn, lead to significant cost and resource requirements to remediate.

The plethora of regulations and approaches actually results in one of the major problems with a quality systems approach. Companies and people are confused and conflicted. There have been so many iterations and experts' personal takes on what to do and how to accomplish it that the quality systems approach has taken on the "latest fad" or "program of the month" moniker. Many companies are hesitant to adopt a quality systems approach because they either are not really certain which concept is the right one, or they are waiting for the next iteration or major breakthrough.

This is a lethal mistake. The old proverb of "he who hesitates is lost" is true. Discussion in later chapters will show why this is so deadly. For now, suffice it to say that usually the resulting death is neither quick nor painless. Most typically, it is a tortured and protracted process that is characterized by an increasingly negative death spiral from which companies may not be able to recover. Companies can literally hemorrhage cash to the point of corporate exsanguination. The companies that have an epiphany and come to the realization they are in serious trouble may not have enough resources and capital to overcome the spiral. They only delay the inevitable. If a company is lucky and catches the problems early enough and has the wherewithal, they may overcome and reverse the spiral.

So remember that for nearly every industry there are agencies and/or organizations that establish rules, regulations, or guidelines. There are also industry accepted practices. I have detailed only a few. You must identify these agencies and organizations that apply to your company as customers so you can understand and meet their requirements.

Key Takeaways

- Identify your regulatory, association, and industry regulations, requirements, and standards.

- Develop a core competency in this area.

- Keep up to date on changes.

- Make certain you meet all applicable requirements.

ENDNOTES

1. Walter A. Shewhart, *Economic Control of Quality of Manufactured Product* (Milwaukee: ASQ Quality Press, 1931).
2. Rafael Aguayo, *Dr. Deming: The American Who Taught the Japanese About Quality* (New York: Fireside, 1991).
3. Kaoru Ishikawa, *Guide to Quality Control (Industrial Engineering & Technology)* (Tokyo: Asian Productivity Organization, 1986).
4. Joseph M. Juran, Frank M. Gryna, ed., *Juran's Quality Control Handbook* (New York: McGraw-Hill, 1988).
5. William Y. Fowlkes and Clyde M. Creveling, *Engineering Methods for Robust Product Design: Using Taguchi Methods in Technology and Product Development* (New York: Prentice Hall, 1995); Philip B. Crosby, *Quality without Tears: The Art of Hassle-Free Management* (New York: McGraw-Hill, 1995); Philip B. Crosby, *Quality Is Free* (New York: Signet, 1980).
6. Hiroyuki Hirano, *JIT Implementation Manual: The Complete Guide to Just-in-Time Manufacturing* (New York: Productivity Press, 1998); Dennis P. Hobbs, *Lean Manufacturing Implementation: A Complete Execution Manual for Any Size Manufacturer* (Alexandria, VA: J. Ross, 2003); Robert S. Kaplan and David P. Norton, *The Strategy-Focused Organization: How Balanced Scorecard Companies Thrive in the New Business Environment* (Boston: Harvard Business School Press, 2000); and Thomas Pyzdek, *The Six Sigma Handbook: The Complete Guide for Greenbelts, Blackbelts, and Managers at All Levels, Revised and Expanded Edition*, 2nd rev. ed. (New York: McGraw-Hill, 2003).
7. http://www.iec.org; http://www.ieee.org; http://www.aami.org; and http://www.ansi.org.
8. http://www.ghtf.org.
9. http://www.ich.org.

3

The Basics of the Approach

Beware of those who come bearing unsolicited gifts. Anyone who comes to you with a package that is not being custom-tailored to your company, culture, and products does not have your best interest at heart. This does not mean that templates and generic requirements are useless. They are often excellent starting points. Just a word of caution: implementing and maintaining a quality system and quality strategy requires work. Most of the time it is a lot of hard work, but well worth the investment in time, energy, and resources. It all starts with your understanding of the requirements necessary for success.

Always remember that a strategic quality system is a neverending drive to identify and understand customers combined with continuous value-added improvement tools and techniques to achieve the highest possible results and returns. The phases of an effective strategic quality system are:

1. Architecture and connections

2. Evaluation and alignment of the elements of the quality system

3. Automation

4. Continuous improvement

In order to establish the basics, an organization, starting at the executive level, must have some prerequisites. Implementation must mean effective implementation. This does not mean just having policies and procedures in place; it means having them effectively developed and utilized on a day-in, day-out basis. Implementation is the most difficult step. It almost always requires integrating a cultural change management aspect with the changed processes and practices. Cultural change here refers to the basic paradigms and practices in place at a company. Changing policies, procedures, and work instructions yields only marginal gains unless the required cultural changes are included.

Accomplishing a cultural change starts at the top of the organization and works its way down. The most difficult position in an organization is line manager. These are the people who actually effect the implementation. They must be effective conduits between top management and the rest of the organization. They must gather and feed the correct information to executive management so that decisions on priorities and resource allocation can be made and the risks may be understood. Line managers must then translate these priorities and resources into effective daily practical applications that keep the business running.

Figure 3.1 depicts the basic process of establishing and maintaining a strategic quality system. The activities are divided into strategic and tactical activities associated with the process. The activities detailed in the darkest boxes represent the four phases of quality systems that are discussed in detail in Chapter 4.

This is a high-level process map establishing the what-to-do requirements for a strategic quality system. This model could be expanded into a series of flowcharts that would detail the specific how-to activities required to establish and maintain your quality system.

Specific flowcharts need to be customized to your particular business and regulatory needs. Therefore, it would be impossible to have detailed flowcharts in this book that would apply to all companies. The basic process details will be explained as you progress through the chapters.

Figure 3.1 shows that there are specific strategic and tactical portions of a quality system. The figure is meant to demonstrate all of the

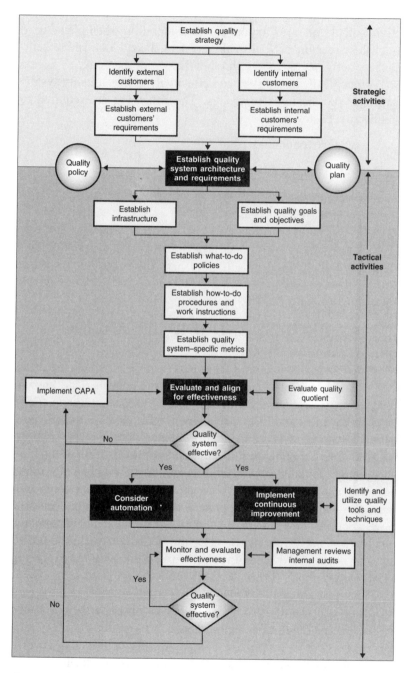

Figure 3.1 Establishing and maintaining a strategic quality system.

activities that you need to take into consideration when planning to establish or reengineer your quality system. Take a look and remember these activities as you go through the rest of the book.

A strategically established and effectively utilized quality system requires a few basic prerequisites. The following are required to establish the basics:

1. Awareness and understanding

2. Commitment and communication

3. Direction and dedication

4. Competency

5. Discipline

These five prerequisites will be discussed in greater detail.

AWARENESS AND UNDERSTANDING

Awareness and understanding seem easy, but, in fact, they are often overlooked in terms of personnel really being educated and knowledgeable regarding strategic quality systems. Executive and functional (department and line) management must have a complete and thorough awareness and appreciation of two things: the customers and how their requirements are integrated into a strategic quality system. It is one thing to have some awareness of a subject, it is quite another to have a substantive working knowledge of the tools and techniques required to demonstrate ability. For example, everyone knows about Albert Einstein, his theory of relativity, and his famous equation $e = mc^2$. How many of us can actually explain the terms and what the equation really is used for, let alone try to explain a black hole?

Customers are one of the keys to the entire strategic quality system. Once you identify and understand your customers, both external and internal, and their requirements, then you can strategically plan your course of action. The course of action will include identification and application of the appropriate tools and techniques to maximize results. This means maximizing results in terms of items such as:

- Highest customer satisfaction and value to the customer

- Highest possible quality at lowest possible cost

- Shortest possible cycle times for processes with highest throughput

This means that management must identify the customers and their requirements including:

- Customers who buy and use your actual products and services

- Applicable regulatory agencies, associations, or industry standards, and the associated requirements

- Internal and external customers who will design, manufacture, service, install, repair, and distribute your products and provide your services

COMMITMENT AND COMMUNICATION

Management must clearly demonstrate its awareness and understanding through commitment and communication. Notice I did not say communicate their awareness. They must demonstrate their understanding and commitment. The cliché of "talk is cheap" applies here. Management must clearly show by its actions that the customer is king and every activity and deliverable is done to meet customer requirements and adds value.

Management cannot insist that subordinates do as they are instructed and then demonstrate by its own actions that exceptions to the systems can be made or the systems can be circumvented to meet business needs. You don't ship questionable products so that the end-of-month or end-of-quarter financials look good, figuring you can always fix the problems in the field. If people see managers allowing themselves exemptions, then they in turn will look to cut every corner and find ingenious work-arounds.

DIRECTION AND DEDICATION

Managers at all levels must translate their awareness and understanding into a well thought-out and measurable strategic plan. This plan must establish activities, deliverables, and measurable objectives by which management and the entire organization will be evaluated. Management must prioritize these and ensure that there are adequate resources (personnel, equipment, facilities, and capital) to effectively accomplish them. Far too often there are conflicting and competing priorities that overstress the resources and ultimately strangle success. Personnel must be given adequate time and resources to accomplish the objectives. If management fails here, confusion reigns, and the company experiences utter confusion and conflicted values. An organization or its personnel cannot thrive or be successful long-term in this condition.

Priorities must be set. Be realistic; how many major projects can your organization actually support and still get products and services out to the customers? It is far better to complete a few selected projects on time, on budget, and effectively, rather than complete several over budget, past schedule, and with marginal effectiveness.

Experience shows that companies generally do not remove projects from peoples' plates, they just give them another plate and expect everything to get done. When things do not get done in a timely or effective manner, the personnel responsible for the projects often face the consequences. Managers must take a long and hard introspective look. If they do this with honesty, they will see the root causes. Most of the time, management's failure to prioritize and allocate resources is what results in organizational disaster. Management must be responsible and accountable and must hold everyone else accountable and responsible for realistic value added to the customer objectives.

COMPETENCY

Competency in several areas is critical to success. Awareness and understanding provide a core of knowledge and skills, but competency means you have people who have proven that they can perform. These are the people who can use Einstein's formula correctly and explain what a black hole is.

The first required competency, management, is divided into two parts: the quality of management and the management of the quality system. Management must have the wherewithal (skills and experience) to know not to micromanage. If micromanagement is required, then the rest of the organization lacks adequate competency and maturity. Executive management must establish the strategy, demonstrate its dedication by prioritizing and allocating resources, and then get out of the way! The only exception is to help resolve problems that cannot be resolved at lower levels.

An organization must have competencies in technical, quality, and business practices in addition to management. Management must determine if the competencies need to be core, part of the infrastructure, or if they can be outsourced.

Good technical (science and/or engineering in development, manufacturing) subject matter experts (SMEs) and support are an absolute must. SMEs are the technical and scientific brain trust. But don't forget the technicians and assistants, as they are the support structure that the SMEs often need to succeed. Quality assurance and personnel who know the applicable regulations and association and industry standard requirements are another essential. They are the mortar in the foundation and bring a needed analytical perspective.

Manufacturing is the engine that gets your products and services out the door. Marketing, sales, distribution, service, accounting, finance, metrology, facilities, human resources, and payroll are also necessary. But these functions are generally more easily outsourced than other functions.

You must determine if these competencies are to be developed and maintained as core, internal competencies or if they can be outsourced.

DISCIPLINE

Last, but certainly not least, is discipline. Management and the organization must have the discipline to know when to say yes and when to say no. Management must demonstrate this discipline if it expects the organization to follow. I am not necessarily advocating a military style of discipline, although for some organizations that works. What

I am saying is that when choices need to be made, they are made and communicated using a risk-based approach so that the entire organization knows that informed decisions are being made. Once the decision is made, the organization focuses on the activities and deliverables required to get the job done effectively and efficiently.

Without discipline, the technical expertise and competency are undermined and oftentimes lost. Consider this example: A company has several complex processes that require process validations. When performing process validations, assure the following:

- Projects are well planned.

- Solid protocols are developed.

- The tests are run and the data gathered.

- Solid statistical analyses are performed and reports are written.

So far so good. The information and documentation are all pulled together and put into a set of three notebooks. An outside auditor comes in to evaluate the process validation. Upon pulling the three notebooks for review, the auditor finds that it is nearly impossible to make sense of the information and documentation. The documentation is not organized in a logical manner, and many of the reports and memos included have handwritten notes, writeovers, and colored sticky notes. Upon further examination of the reports, the auditor finds that extensive testing and inspection were conducted and hundreds of data points gathered and analyzed. Four test results that were outside the specifications were excluded from the study.

While eventually getting some people to come and explain the information and data, the auditor is not happy with the results. Why? The lack of discipline to make the information and data self-explanatory and stand-alone detract from the good science and technical work that was done. Similarly, the exclusion of data also shows a lack of discipline, not to mention potential ethical and legal implications.

This is why you must have the discipline to know what the right things to do are and the discipline to do them. You must also have the discipline to hire and retain the best people you can get and to weed out the underachievers.

RISK-BASED ANALYSIS

A risk-based approach takes into account a variety of factors:

- Safety risks to patients and customers
- Quality and reliability risks to products and services
- Regulatory risks
- Business risks in terms of schedule, cost, and resources

Figure 3.2 shows these four basic risks. The first risks to consider are the safety risks, as these are the highest impact. Safety risks may result in harm to users of your products. They are generally higher in severity, but may vary greatly in their probability of occurrence.

If you do not understand the terms *risk analysis* and *risk management,* these are something you must learn. These are basic tools that you must have as part of the core management, technical, and quality competencies.

Then come the quality risks. These are the quality and reliability risks. Something along the lines of "the good news is that all of the products your company sells meet all of your specifications . . . the

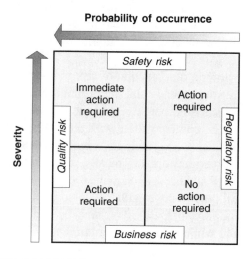

Figure 3.2 Risk-based analysis.

bad news is that your customers experience a five percent out-of-box failure rate." These risks are generally higher in probability, but the severity may be varied. These risks may not cause harm to your customers, but they certainly can shut your business down. These risks result in rework, scrap, the inability to provide products due to back orders, and the like.

Next consider the regulatory-related risks. These are the risks that impact your regulatory, association, and industry standards requirements. These could result in recalls of products or more serious regulatory and legal consequences. Regulatory risks are generally low in probability, although this may vary greatly depending on the state of your quality system. Regulatory risks may also vary greatly in severity.

Last come the business risks. All of the other risks can be translated into business risks because everything comes down to the bottom line. How does each of these risks translate into costs: expense, capital, facilities, resource consumption, and so on? Business risk is not less important than others. In fact, all of the risks have the potential to shut down or severely impact your company.

The more mature and effective your quality system, the lower the individual and overall risks. This is because you should be proactively identifying and mitigating/eliminating risk. The probability of issues occurring and the severity of issues will be lowered proportionally to the level of understanding and implementing risk management.

Figure 3.2 shows a fundamental of risk management. If the risk (a combination of the severity and the probability that an event will or has happened) starts to increase, then the immediacy and level of response needs to be commensurate with the risk. Taking this a step further, all potential or actual safety risks require some action, usually immediate and sometimes drastic (recalls, removals, or withdrawals of products, or medical intervention to prevent or treat injured patients and/or users). All other risks (regulatory, quality, and business) may require action, and some of these actions may be significant and require immediate action; while others may require considerably less action and less immediacy.

I bring up risk because a major part of the strategic approach to a quality system is setting up a risk-based approach to identify and analyze customer information. This in turn ensures that adequate and appropriate decisions at the management level can be made regarding priorities and resource allocation.

This all leads to risk management, not just the traditional fault tree analyses or failure mode and effects analyses that are typically done for products.[1] This is risk-based management at the business level as well as risk management at the product level. This all leads to making proactive risk management pay off.[2]

All of these risks must be evaluated to determine the impact of the decision. If the risk is understood and acceptable, then proceed. If not, have the discipline to say no. Have the discipline to find out the real root causes of issues and then to get them fixed. Don't put a bandage on it, get to the root and fix it.

Key Takeaways

- Understand that there are four phases of an effective strategic quality system:

  - Architecture and connections

  - Evaluation and alignment

  - Automation

  - Continuous improvement

- Understand and apply the basics:

  - Awareness and understanding

  - Commitment and communication

  - Direction and dedication

  - Competency

  - Discipline

ENDNOTES

1. Richard E. Barlow, *Reliability and Fault Tree Analysis* (Detroit, MI: Society for Industrial and Applied Mathematics, 1982); and Dean H. Stamatis, *Failure Mode and Effects Analysis: FMEA from Theory to Execution* (Milwaukee: ASQ Quality Press, 2003).
2. Thomas L. Barton, William G. Shenkir, and Paul L. Walker, *Making Enterprise Risk Management Pay Off: How Leading Companies Implement Risk Management* (New York: Financial Times Prentice Hall, 2002).

4

The Four Phases of Quality Systems

The first prerequisite of a quality system is that it must be driven by customer requirements. Therefore, if you make absolutely certain that your quality system is driven by customers, this will ensure the correct perspective and practices.

Having said that, every company I have worked for or with has said that it knows who its customers are, and can give you a list. Upon further examination and evaluation, the majority do not include the applicable regulatory agencies, associations, or industry standards organizations as their customers. They have actually failed to identify a major player as a customer. This represents a major business risk. Many companies also do not consider the internal customers when designing, developing, implementing, and maintaining the quality system. This is also a major risk.

If you fail to do this adequately and effectively, you will find that you are headed down a path that will be wrought with higher costs, lengthier implementation cycles, and suboptimal efficiency. Your quality system maintenance costs will also be higher because you will iterate and reiterate the processes, trying to bring them to an optimal state. If you fail to optimize your quality system, you will incur additional costs year after year. Also, if you fail to optimize your quality system, you will experience inefficiencies, which lead to nonconformances, which lead to increased regulatory and business risks.

Your organization may already be a significant way down the path of accomplishing the activities just listed. If so, then examine your quality system and ensure that the four phases have been put in proper order.

The second prerequisite is that the requirements be integrated with appropriate tools and techniques to drive and maximize continuous improvement. These two combined create synergies that each alone cannot accomplish.

The four phases of quality systems must be integrated, and these are far more difficult to implement concurrently. The four phases of the quality system include:

- Architecture and connections

- Evaluation and alignment

- Automation

- Continuous improvement

Building architecture and integrating the elements must come first. Those who develop products and services will understand this because you cannot make the right products or provide the right services unless and until you have identified the requirements and specifications. That is precisely what building architecture and integrating elements are. They are the translation of requirements (needs) into specifications for infrastructure, resources, systems, and practices. Figure 4.1 shows the relationship between the four phases and the mandatory link to the customers.

BUILD ARCHITECTURE AND CONNECTIONS

The first building block of the architecture is the organization infrastructure (people)—what kind and how many. It is absolutely essential that your organization have people who (1) are focused on customers (to implement and maintain the quality system), (2) have a proactive mentality, (3) know your culture (either the current culture, if that is what you want, or the future state), and (4) have the necessary skills sets to be successful.

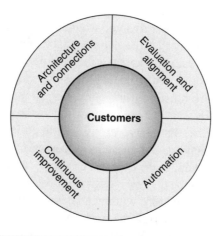

Figure 4.1 The four phases of quality systems.

The second set of building blocks consists of the processes and systems. It is interesting to note the relationship between people and processes. Experience demonstrates time and again that average people can be successful given excellent processes; similarly, excellent people can be successful with average processes. Average people combined with excellent processeses will outperform excellent people with average processeses. Average people are not successful with average practices.

Think of children playing baseball. At age six, a single outstanding player can dominate and win. Now look at high school or college teams. Every player is highly skilled. Certainly there are still the outstanding players, but they are less likely to dominate. Even at the professional level, outstanding starting pitchers only pitch every fourth or fifth day, outstanding batters only come to the plate to hit four or five times a game. Having one or two outstanding players does not guarantee wins, a winning season, or a World Series ring. It is extremely rare for a team with one all-star to win a championship. Even Michael Jordan had a good supporting team and a great coach.

Don't get me wrong, you want as many talented and outstanding people as you can get and afford; they certainly make an impact. But business is a team sport, and each member of your team must come prepared to play every day. You also need people who know how to get the most out of the team.

The obvious premise is that you want both good players and good managers. This means that the people establishing and maintaining the quality system must understand the customers' needs and translate them into effective and efficient processes, practices, and systems. It also means there must be trust, communication, and commitment (remember Chapter 2?). The only way to create real synergies between people and processes is to have strong people utilizing well thought-out, clear, user-friendly, and efficient processes and systems.

Architecture includes the policies, processes, and systems that will be the foundation of the quality system in terms of day-to-day practices and culture. The connections within and between the elements of your quality system are critical for its proper functioning.

Think of your computer system. It is composed of some basic elements: hard drive, disk drive, memory, printer, and keyboard. Without the cables that provide the connections within and among these elements, how can the computer work, let alone be effective and efficient? Without software, the hardware is pretty useless. There must be connections within and between the hardware elements, and there must also be connections/interfaces between the hardware and the software. The connections will be covered after the basic structural elements have been discussed.

In addition to the elements of the quality system, architecture also includes building the correct and adequate facilities and infrastructure to support and nurture the quality system. Chapter 6 on competencies will help define the requirements for the right personnel to have in terms of skill sets. As stated earlier, but worth stating again, meeting the external customers' needs will ensure that the correct elements are in your quality system; meeting the internal customers' needs will ensure that your quality system is effective and efficient.

The architecture of the quality system is further divided into another set of six building blocks, as shown in Figure 4.2. In Chapter 1, four major subsystems were identified: management, corrective and preventive action, documentation and change management, and design control. These were mentioned as the major subsystems because they are the systems that are most directly connected to the external customers who use your products and services. Production and process controls and facilities, utilities, and equipment are now added because they most directly impact the internal

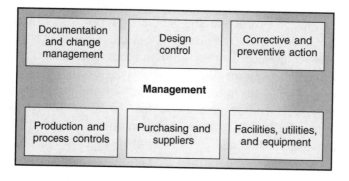

Figure 4.2   Quality system elements.

customers. Additionally, purchasing and suppliers are added because they link you to suppliers to whom you are customers.

Part of identifying and understanding customer requirements is to understand that every relationship is a customer–supplier relationship, and you will not always be the supplier. The key is knowing to whom you are the supplier and exactly what it is you supply. For example, if you deal with regulatory agencies, do you supply them products? Not usually, but you do supply them with information necessary to show you understand and meet their requirements. This information and documentation makes you the supplier, so they must be the customers.

These six building blocks are all held together by the seventh element—management practices and systems. These management practices and systems provide the mortar for the quality system. The blocks are all the same color, size, and shape. Because they are like bricks in a foundation, each carries equal weight and is equally important to the establishment and maintenance of your quality system.

This does not mean that management must micromanage the entire business. The opposite is actually true. Management must macromanage the systems, practices, and people; management must provide adequate leadership, direction, and oversight. Experience has shown that detail-oriented, hands-on, in-your-face management is actually counterproductive and negatively impacts both the effectiveness and the efficiency of the quality system.

The way to ensure that you get the right people is to start with the expectations. In the requirements for each position: (1) define the customer requirements for the position (both external and internal), (2) establish the activities and responsibilities for the position based on the requirements, and (3) get people with the right experience, education, and background. Look for the most highly talented people you can find, hire them, and retain them.

If management is micromanaging, that is a clear indication that there is something wrong. Either the personnel are not right—based on the criteria just listed—or management personnel may not be the right people. As stated previously, management must lead, direct, challenge, and provide oversight.

This requires that management drive the quality system by utilizing a risk-based approach to setting priorities and allocating resources. Management must ensure that the quality system can and does identify, gather, and collate micro-level data and information so that management can in turn combine this with macro-level, risk-based analyses to establish priorities and allocate resources.

Management at many companies mistakenly thinks they are doing this. They are gathering data. They are looking at charts and graphs, but they are not setting priorities and allocating resources in a manner that drives true synergies and effectiveness.

These companies become the world's greatest firefighters. They tend to be reactive and focus on product issues. They do not realize, often until too late, that they are no longer winning the firefighting battle because they have been hobbled by years of continuously jumping from fire to fire and not taking any true preventive actions. Prevention is the key.

If your company has more priorities than people, *you have a problem.* If priorities are not ranked correctly, *you have a problem.* If you have problems with your external customers (either patients, users, or regulatory agencies), *you have a problem.* And the problem is mainly management. I am not bashing management, because good management is necessary. Management must know what and how to manage just as SMEs must know how and when to use the their technical expertise.

Based on experience, management is the only part of the quality system where people can actually be the problem. If the right people are not in management, then the rest of the quality system, regardless of how bright, dedicated, and committed management is, will not ultimately be successful. If the right people are in management, the rest of the system will be driven by the right requirements.

Management must be accountable for and hold others accountable for the quality system. By this, I mean that management must ultimately take ownership for the quality system, which includes establishing and maintaining the architecture, infrastructure, connections, alignment, evaluation, automation, and continuous improvement. Holding others accountable is accomplished by: (1) getting and retaining adequate numbers of trained and dedicated employees and supporting them with other non-personnel resources, and (2) having them identify and resolve issues at the system level.

The result will be that issues, problems, and nonconformances that arise will be addressed at and by the systems. For example, the right people will be matched to the right jobs, and people in the wrong jobs will be reassigned to appropriate jobs or retrained and put in the right jobs. If an employee is having too much rework and scrap, it is because the employee has not been trained adequately, is not being supervised adequately, or was hired into the wrong job. These are all system problems, not employee problems.

This sounds like business heresy, but more often than not, management is either *the* leading root cause or one of the leading root causes of the problems associated with establishing and maintaining a strategic quality system. This is because management fails to:

- Hire, reward, and retain the right people.

- Make certain that people are in the right jobs and functions.

- Get rid of the people who impede or do not positively contribute.

- Recognize that managers themselves may be the wrong people.

- Make the tough, but honest, introspective analyses, evaluations, and decisions.

- Proactively and realistically prioritize projects.

- Adequately obtain and allocate resources.

Here are some examples of management being the root cause of quality system problems:

• Company A fails to hire a truly gifted engineer because the salary cap is $85,000 per year, and the engineer wants $90,000. This engineer has a proven history of contribution and teamwork, and the savings this engineer could provide versus a lower-level performer could easily yield a return on the extra $5,000 within months.

• Company B has a scientist who has incredible intuitive insight. He can figure things out that most people haven't even thought of yet. He is, however, an arrogant, noncommunicative introvert who doesn't share information, views knowledge as power, and, as a result, doesn't document his work adequately. The company's solution for handling the situation was to transfer him to position after position rather than address the real root cause issues.

• Company C has a manager who micromanages everyone in the department. The manager insists on doing things her way and changes peoples' priorities and projects on a daily basis. The company's solution: rather than counsel, coach, or correct the problem, the manager was promoted to director where she can now negatively impact a much larger portion of the company.

• Company D has had five negative regulatory inspections and three warning letters in the past four years. The solution: Executive management moved the operations director to quality and the quality director to operations at another site. A new operations manager was hired at the original site signifying "under new management." Executives also fired two engineers and an auditor and laid off three supervisors and four inspectors. The next inspection six months later resulted in a fourth warning letter and a threat of further action.

• Management at Company E prioritizes the 54 existing projects and objectives and assigns responsibility for each. In reviewing the results, most projects are either over budget, past schedule, or not effective (the old "80 percent of the projects get 20 percent done and 20 percent of the projects get 80 percent done" syndrome). The solution: everyone is now working 60-hour weeks, but more projects are assigned and nothing is taken off peoples' plates. The result: same old same old.

These are only a few examples of management's failure to manage the quality system effectively.

This is why it is so important to get people with the right skill sets into the organization and to establish compensation and career paths that will ensure their retention and continued contribution. Progression planning is another practice management often fails to develop adequately: Identify the key people, plan for their success and promotion, and plan for their replacements.

A few words on training. Identify the training and development needs for everyone in the organization. All training must have measurable effectiveness checks built in. This means that part of training includes setting metrics to be monitored to determine the effectiveness of the training. This should be done both short and long term. You must understand the difference between the different types of training: awareness based, knowledge based, and skill based.[1] The different levels of training require different levels of effectiveness checks.

Remember the discussion of Einstein? Do you need to be aware of who he was and what he did? Or know his formulas and concepts and where they apply? Or be able to actually use the formulas and calculate the speed of light using them?

Quality System Architecture and Connections

You may be asking, "What does all of this have to do with quality systems?" That is a fair question. The answer is, the right people are the key to strategically planning, establishing, and maintaining the quality system. This includes management and nonmanagement people as well. If only management plans the quality system, it will not be nearly as effective or efficient as if people throughout the organization planned it. The old adage of, "People don't plan to fail, but do fail to plan," or plan adequately, holds true. Failure to strategically plan is as fatal as failing to build the right products or provide the right services. This includes planning the strategic and tactical aspects of the quality system from the beginning. It also means having the discipline to follow the plan. If the plan isn't working, it means having the courage and foresight to take that introspective look and make the necessary changes.

Strategic planning includes identifying and establishing all quality system requirements, then establishing a method to accomplish these requirements. That gives a pretty good exposé on the people and management aspects of architecture. The next part of the architecture involves establishing (remember, this means define, document, and effectively implement) the following:

- Systems (policies, practices, and processes)

- Flowcharts and process maps

- Procedures (standard operating procedures, work instructions, and forms)

These must flow from the top down in terms of starting with the policies and then working into the procedures and forms. You may be able to accomplish this concurrently, but it is hard to imagine how to define the process or procedure until the basic policies are established.

Figure 4.3 shows the basic architecture of the quality system that most successful companies have utilized. It starts with the mission/vision and progressively translates it into what to do and how to do it through policies and procedures at varying levels; depending on the size, nature, and complexity of your organization and products.

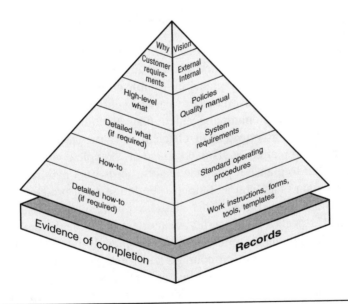

Figure 4.3   Quality system architecture.

Figure 4.4 details an integrated quality system. It includes the core business and quality system processes needed to establish the basic infrastructure. Look at the architecture in Figure 4.3 and the content

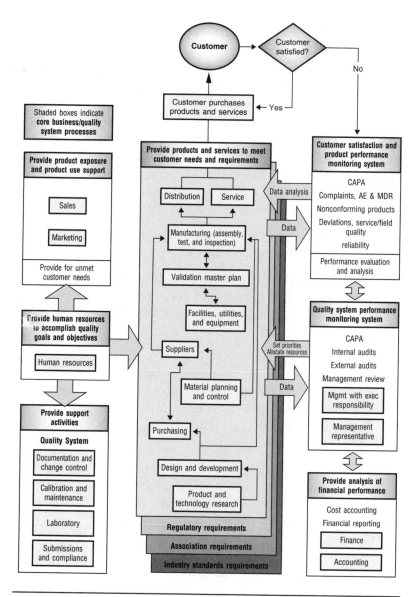

Figure 4.4 An integrated quality system.

of Figure 4.4 and make certain that you have adequately addressed each item in Figure 4.4 at both the policy *what* level and the procedural *how* level. Don't forget the forms—especially important in a regulated industry. The level of detail required for a large multinational, multifacility corporation is significantly different than for a small start-up. The elements are the same, but the detail may be very different.

Management Architecture and Connections

In either situation, management has some significant decisions to make. What is the appropriate balance between enough architecture to make certain everyone works toward the same policies and enough flexibility to accommodate different facilities, geographies, personnel, and products? Organizations must decide the ever-present issue of centralized versus decentralized. They must ask:

- Is a single corporate level of policies that establishes the basic architecture adequate?

- Are corporate procedures needed? If so, then realize this may require that your facilities are more like McDonalds where everything is exactly the same. This may be what you need, but it may create some incredible hardships on the facilities.

- Do you want to have the corporate policies provide architecture and allow a more entrepreneurial approach at the site and facility level in order to provide flexibility at the procedural level?

All companies wrestle with the same concepts, but at different levels of impact. The main thing with all companies is to plan for the future, rather than react to it when it becomes the present. Successful companies have short-term, intermediate, and long-term financial plans. Start thinking about where you will be in three to five or five to 10 years, and the architecture needed for that goal. Keep in mind that regulatory requirements change over time just as product and customer requirements do. Focus on being proactive and investing for a successful future. Too many companies wait until they have a customer problem: either a field action for products or some form of regulatory agency intervention. It is always more costly to be reactive than proactive.

All of these decisions should be made utilizing a risk-based approach. Examine and evaluate the risks and benefits of each approach and pick the one with the lowest risk or lowest residual risk.

Make certain that the internal customers are involved in the decisions and in the planning. This will ensure that their requirements are considered adequately and lead to a more effective and efficient system. This assumes, of course, that you have the right people.

Once all of these decisions and considerations have been made, management can then prioritize the activities, assign the deliverables, set the time frame, and allocate the resources. Failure to plan all of this adequately in the beginning will result in increased cost, time, and problems. It is important to be reminded that inefficiency leads to errors, which lead to nonconformances, which, in turn, lead to increased regulatory and business risks and costs.

Now considerations for the architecture of the other six building blocks can be evaluated. These come after the personnel and management architecture because, as stated previously, without the right people, the quality system cannot be established adequately in terms of effectiveness and efficiency.

The following sections contain the basics that need to be included in the architecture for the six building-block elements.

Additional Management Considerations

Management architecture is, as stated previously, the mortar that holds the quality system together. Without the right ingredients, the mortar is useless—at least long-term. Your organization may get by in the short term, but over the long term, things will start to fall apart.

The following are some of the essential ingredients required for the management mortar. These are in addition to having the correct management personnel.

A successful organization is based on management's accountability for the quality system and holding everyone in the organization accountable for the quality system. This often means changing the culture, starting at the top. One way to get the attention of people (throughout the organization) is to tie compensation (merit increases, bonuses, and so on) directly to quality system effectiveness. Establish three to five key quality system effectiveness metrics and set goals, and hold people accountable by measuring and monitoring the metrics. You will be surprised how much attention you get when you affect people in the pocketbook.

Establish ongoing, strategic quality planning.[2] Just as you do financial planning, spend the same amount of time and effort planning your quality system activities for the year. Plan for where you want your organization to be in the future. Adopt the attitude that the level of quality may be good or even excellent, but that it is never good enough: there are always things to be improved. Determine what metrics are needed in order to ensure customer satisfaction (both external and internal) and drive your quality system in that direction. Also review and critique the quality system plan with the same detail and frequency that you do for your company's financial plan. The quality health of the company is a good indicator of its financial health. Have short-term, intermediate, and long-term plans that are meaningful and realistic.

Establish specific metrics. Notice the use of metrics, not objectives. This does not mean you shouldn't have objectives. Objectives are necessary, but more times than not, objectives are ambiguous and not clearly measurable. Specific metrics are used to monitor the real progress or lack thereof within the quality system. Too many organizations appear to have objectives without meaningful metrics.

For example, an objective is to increase customer satisfaction by 10 percent. Seems measurable, right? Wrong. This must be defined further to be meaningful. What is a 10 percent increase? Is it 10 percent fewer complaints, 10 percent fewer out-of-box failures, 10 percent more sales, or 10 percent more revenue? Ambiguous, unclear, and conflicting objectives only create chaos and inefficiency.

Executive management must make certain that there are not too many objectives and metrics. The system can be paralyzed by too much information and data. People can only handle so much work. Establish a system to identify objectives, prioritize them, and then translate them into specific metrics. Based on experience, the most successful companies load their people to about 85 percent capacity.[3] This allows flexibility for emergencies or increased requirements. Many companies (again, based on experience) have people working 50-plus-hour weeks and keep loading them with additional work (objectives and projects) without any relief. This is a good way to lose the highest contributors. You just burn them out.

So much time has been spent here on management because it is often the most overlooked part of the quality system. Companies figure they have the top MBAs and such in management, so they must be able to run the company. This is not always the case. Do not get me wrong, top MBAs are highly valuable and sought after, and rightly so. Many of these people have uncanny business acumen. They do not, however, all have the same level of quality systems acumen.

To reiterate because of the importance of this, management is the only area within the quality system where personnel can actually be the root cause of the problem. This is because management is responsible for getting the quality system effectively established and maintained. Having the right people in place to do this is critical; having the wrong people in place can be a disaster. In actuality, even management personnel issues are system issues. It is just that because of their responsibilities and authority, the impact is much broader and more evident with management than with personnel in other positions.

For all other aspects of the quality system, people are not the problem, the systems are the problem. Management is responsible for the systems and the people who will establish and maintain them. If you have a problem that you think is people related, I challenge you to do a more thorough and introspective evaluation and analysis. Experience has shown time and time again that problems are related to systems, not to individuals. The following is a list of examples that are often identified, incorrectly, as people problems:

- The system to identify, hire, reward, and retain the right people has resulted in someone being in the wrong job and performing poorly.

- Training and education of personnel so they know what the right things are and do them correctly has resulted in someone who routinely exceeds the process cycle times, leading to backlogs in production.

- Training supervisory staff on oversight and discipline has resulted in a manufacturing line with excessive scrap and rework.

- Having people who are trained and committed to
  identifying the specific related systems issues and getting
  them fixed, resulting in systems that are not followed
  so people develop their own systems, which are not
  adequately documented.

Individuals not performing are the results/effects of inadequate systems, not the root causes.

Management has two basic responsibilities in a strategic quality system: first, set and communicate priorities, and, second, allocate adequate resources to ensure that the priorities are successfully (effectively and efficiently) completed. This is obviously a bit of an oversimplification. It includes planning, setting objectives, a certain level of oversight, and several other activities. These are all aimed, however, at gathering the correct information to make the priority and resource allocation decisions to assure that the quality system is effectively implemented and maintained. Management must be the champion and sponsor of and for the quality system.

Next, establish the management representative. This is the quality system ambassador and ombudsperson who acts as the conduit from the heart of the organization to management and vice versa. This person must have the skills and ability to monitor the quality system and to communicate concepts and values up and down the organizational architecture. This person must have the ear of the highest members of executive management, and trust and respect at all levels in the organization.

The management representative interfaces with management, executive management, and functional directors, managers, and supervisors to gather and analyze quality data. This requires that the management representative have a combination of skills: management, technical, team building, quality assurance, and, probably most important, outstanding communication and presentation skills.

Also establish the eyes and ears of management, otherwise known as audits. In a regulated industry you are required to have audits. You should also make certain that your internal audit system is built around assessment. This does not mean that you do not audit; audits generally provide greater depth and detail. Audits, however, have a negative connotation of being witch hunts and fault finding missions, deservedly so, since they focus on nonconformances.

Assessments have a dual focus: to recognize and leverage what is working well in addition to finding areas for improvement. Keep in mind that your audits and assessments are only as good as the system (practices and procedures) and the people who perform them. You want your internal audits to be the most rigorous evaluation of activities and documentation that your personnel will ever encounter. Too many times internal audits and auditors are either rough and gruff or they are not taken seriously. Internal audits/assessments are an opportunity for people to run things by the auditors as well. Not just anyone can be an auditor. It takes technical, systems, and communications skills tied together with the persistent inquisitiveness of Sherlock Holmes.

While there are cases to be made for regulatory agency–style internal audits, experience has shown that highly interactive internal audits discover and end up resolving more issues. Interactive audits/assessments also build trust and respect between the auditors and the auditees.

Your audit program can serve both purposes without creating redundant activities. Teach your auditors to assess as well as audit. The goal of assessing and auditing is to identify areas for improvement and then to ensure that the improvements are effectively made in a timely manner. Create audit checklists and review/revise them every audit cycle.

Make certain that everyone in the organization has adequate training, education, and experience. Establish job descriptions/requirements that are translated into training needs. Then establish the training programs and document the training. All training must have some type of knowledge, proficiency, and/or effectiveness measures to ensure that people do more than simply read a manual or sit through the training.

The key takeaways for management are:

- Get the right people.

- Prioritize projects.

- Allocate resources (people, facilities, equipment, capital, and so on).

- Ensure that an effective quality system is established and maintained.

Examples of Not-So-Good and Good Practices

At this point, pause to consider the following two examples.[4] You might identify with one of these examples. If not, consider which is the good practice and which is the not-so-good practice example.

Incredible Concepts Corporation (ICC) is a relatively large multinational corporation (annual sales in excess of $1 billion) that makes several cutting-edge life supporting and sustaining products that also have several disposable accessories. ICC has three manufacturing facilities in the United States and three more in Europe. Development is done at one facility in the United States and one in Europe. ICC has just gotten a new CEO who has a history of success as a motivational leader and a hands-on style for getting companies to perform financially. The CEO has an MBA from a well-known university and is incredibly gifted in terms of being able to motivate people emotionally to get things done. The CEO has a very strong marketing, sales, and operations background. The management staff consists of vice presidents of finance and new product development and directors of quality, regulatory, human resources, and materials.

The CEO spends over 80 percent of the time in the plant and communicating with the facilities making certain that manufacturing gets the products made and shipped. To this end, the CEO is in charge of manufacturing and distribution. Additional management staff is in place for the other operations. These positions are all highly experienced ICC veterans who have all come up through the ranks and report directly to the CEO. Decisions go directly to the CEO for approval.

Management reviews are conducted every six months, and they discuss the manufacturing results (including rework and scrap), shipping results (including back orders and wrong shipments), and the customary financial and budget information for each facility.

Internal audits are conducted annually at each facility; additionally, a corporate audit is performed at each facility. Resulting nonconformances are reported directly to the CEO.

Perfect Products, Inc. (PPI) is a slightly smaller company ($350 million in sales) that develops and manufactures an extensive line of fairly high-volume commercial and personal disposable products. It has two facilities in the United States, one in Europe, one in Japan, and one in Australia. The CEO spends about 60 percent to 65 percent of the time out in the field with field service and sales personnel and with customers. The management team is composed of a mix of both experienced and relatively young professionals, several from other industries. The management team consists of directors who all have strong educational (technical and/or business) and/or experience-based backgrounds.

The management team is responsible for coordinating with the site management teams to oversee the day-to-day activities at the various facilities. It has developed specific plans, objectives, and critical metrics that are used to evaluate the company's performance. Decisions are made by the management team. Development is conducted at the headquarters in the United States and then transferred to the selected manufacturing sites.

Management reviews at each site are conducted monthly and reported to the PPI management team. The team reviews the performance using the objectives and critical metrics for each facility. A quarterly management review is conducted reviewing the performance at each site and PPI as a whole.

Internal audits are performed annually at each facility, and an annual corporate audit is performed at each facility. The results are reported to the management of the affected facility. The management team reviews the results at the management reviews.

Ask yourself which of these is the good and which is the not-so-good. Why? In reading through this book so far you should come to the realization that PPI is generally the better of the two companies. It still has some areas for improvement, possibly significant improvement, but it follows the basics better.

Corrective and Preventive Action Architecture and Connections

Corrective and preventive action (CAPA) is used to identify, gather, collate, and analyze data and information that can be utilized by management to make decisions about priorities and resource allocation. It functions like the central processing unit of a computer. It must have a broad scope. Every element of your quality system must feed data and information into the CAPA engine. If this is not the case, you are in for problems.

A brief explanation of CAPA is warranted here. Corrective actions are reactive actions taken to correct a problem that has already occurred. For example, a lot of widgets failed the bonding inspection criteria. The corrective actions may include rework and reinspection or scrap. Preventive actions are those proactive actions taken to eliminate the causes of potential problems (nonconformances and defects). In the widget example, this would be figuring out the true root cause(s) and getting it fixed so that further problems are eliminated before they happen. Both corrective and preventive actions can involve processes and business practices; preventive actions almost always do.

Make certain that customer complaints (including adverse events and medical device reports for FDA-regulated companies) feed into the CAPA system. All sources of quality system data, metrics, and problems must feed into the CAPA system for evaluation. The CAPA system has two main goals using these data, metrics, and problems information: to identify individual events or issues that require CAPA and to identify trends of events or issues that require CAPA.

Every CAPA must have an adequate effectiveness check to make certain that the right problem was identified and resolved. Many times companies think the following is an example of adequate CAPA: A customer complaint is received that says a product did not perform as expected. The root cause is identified as a specific component in a specific lot of product. The component is changed out, and manufacturing is notified of the change. The quality assurance department checks to make certain that the specifications have been changed and that the new components are being used. Quality assurance even looks to make certain that the customer complaints for that component are reduced, and they are. End of story.

It should *not* be the end of the story. The CAPA system needs to look within and between products, functions, and sites for similar issues. It must also evaluate the totality of the quality system to determine any additional issues. For example:

- Are there any other products that use that component? Do they have any issues?

- Why was this not picked up in the design risk analyses? If it was, why was it not acted upon?

- Are there other issues/problems with this product? Is this the only problem or have there been others? What has been done about them?

The real issue may well be in the design control system, and that was not even addressed in the original CAPA.

The CAPA system must have a comprehensive root cause analysis mechanism that will get to the real root cause.[5] This process requires rigor and vigor. Your organization must be willing to look for the real root cause and accept the sometimes painful truths that are revealed.

The CAPA system must include and be executed by personnel with adequate technical knowledge of your products and services, analytical methods (Pareto, regression analysis, and so on), root cause analysis, and risk-based analyses. The CAPA information must come from every element within your quality system and feed directly into management (both at the functional and the executive levels) for review, analysis, and action. The CAPA system must include issues (events and trends) for:

- Management review

- Audit issues (internal, third-party, and regulatory agency)

- Manufacturing (nonconforming product, rework, scrap, in-process and finished goods testing and inspection, handling, storage, and so on)

- Process deviations and nonconformances

- Field (complaints, servicing, out-of-box failures, shipping, order processing, and so on)

- Purchasing (supplier performance, incoming products, purchase order errors, and so on)

Use the CAPA system as the starting point of your continuous improvement processes. CAPA provides the data and information that are used proactively to improve practices, processes, and products. Figure 4.5 can be used to identify risks and benefits and to make informed decisions. Any issue can be evaluated for these basic considerations to determine the risk/benefit analysis.

Issue to evaluate	Current state risks	Current state benefits	Future state risks	Future state benefits	Comments
Short-term impact on customers (Supply, quality, reliability, and value)	↑↓−[1]	↑↓−[1]	↑↓−[1]	↑↓−[1]	[2]
Long-term impact on customers					
Regulatory impact (Compliance and submissions)					
Impact on quality system (Value-added or not)					
Project cycle time/schedule					
Project resources requirements (Personnel, capital, equipment)					
Short-term financial/ revenue impact (Cost of quality [price of conformance and nonconformance])					
Long-term financial/ revenue impact					

Note 1 Indicate if the risk(s) or benefit(s) are increasing, decreasing, or stable.

Note 2 Include comments regarding root cause(s) or risk(s) and associated cost(s). Also include comments regarding investment costs and ROI to move to future state and reduce risk.

Figure 4.5   Business risk table.

With Figure 4.5 it becomes easier to see if the benefits outweigh the risks and if the risks are acceptable. Either way, you can make informed decisions regarding the size, scope, and impact of projects. This can also be effective in prioritizing the projects.

The major takeaway for CAPA is to remember that it is the element that gathers, analyzes, and investigates all of the quality data from all of the elements of the quality system. Also keep in mind that just because the CAPA function is gathering and evaluating all of these data, it does not mean that every item requires CAPA. The CAPA system needs to be set up to handle three situations:

1. Is any individual event serious enough to require CAPA? If you have one lot of product that has increased rejects due to a caliper being out of calibration, do you need to initiate a CAPA for that lot? Not necessarily, the lot can be reinspected with calibrated calipers. You will, however, need to evaluate the calipers and see if there are additional issues (other lots affected, other calipers affected, and root cause for the out-of-calibration) that may require CAPA.

2. Is there a trend of data that indicates a systemic problem? You should slice and dice data within and between products, production lines, facilities, departments, and so on, to see if there are any trends. Sometimes the low frequency of occurrences are actually the tip of an iceberg. You will not know unless you are on the lookout.

3. Is there a trend of information that indicates that there is an opportunity for continuous improvement? Are there data showing that you can reduce cycle times, increase throughputs, and so on. You may be getting engineering changes completed in five days. Investigation of system data may indicate that with some readjustments of the process you could trim an additional day off of the process cycle time.

Examples of Not-So-Good and Good Practices

ICC has had three instances of manufacturing problems with one of their products at the U.S. manufacturing plant. The problem relates to an automated test that is utilized for process testing of the printed circuit board used in the final product. This has resulted in an increase in the rework rate from one percent to six percent over the past three weeks. The CEO is leading a team to find the problem and get it fixed. The same automated test is used in the European facility that also manufactures the same product. The European facility has not experienced the problem. There, the team is composed of the CEO and two engineers. They come to the conclusion that it must be a sensor in the test equipment; upon removal of the sensor it is determined that it has failed. The sensor was due for maintenance within three weeks anyway, so the team decides to replace the sensor and restart the process.

At PPI, one of the manufacturing engineers has noticed that one the sensors on the automated testing stations has required replacement before its regularly scheduled maintenance. This has occurred on two different automated test stations at one of the facilities that makes tubing sets. A team is pulled together that includes the manufacturing engineer, a development engineer, a manufacturing technician who runs the stations, and a quality engineer.

The team determines that the sensors are being over-torqued and this is causing premature failure. The immediate correction is to replace the sensor, recalibrate the test station, and restart production. The team has also reviewed the process risk analysis and seen that this was not identified on the risk analysis. The team updates the risk analysis and also notifies the engineers at all of the facilities about this new item. In addition to this, the team decides to check the other sensors in the automated test stations at all of the facilities that have the same automated test stations. It also puts in place a project to check the torque of all the sensors and to retrain all of the technicians that maintain the automated test stations. As a result, an engineering change order is created to update the equipment and sensor specifications and the maintenance and equipment troubleshooting procedures.

Design Control Architecture and Connections

The goal here is to gather the customer requirements in order to make products customers want to buy rather than trying to sell them what you have made and to create processes that your organization can and will use. Establish a customer-focused design and development system. This means that products and services are based on external customer (patients and users) requirements and that processes for manufacturing (assembly, test, and inspection) are based on the internal customers' requirements. Regulatory agency and technical organization requirements can be applicable to both the products and the manufacturing processes, so identify their requirements and incorporate them into the product/process requirements.

Your design and development process should be established as a series of transitions:

- Customer requirements to setting specifications

- Specifications to prototypes and pilots

- Prototypes and pilots to full manufacturing

Make certain that all development activities are adequately documented. In a regulated environment, inadequate documentation can lead to some real regulatory and business risks: delayed or denied approvals, additional work, or repeat design validation and design verification. It is critical to have clear gates/handoffs between research and development and between development and commercialization/ manufacturing.

Design-transfer checklists (from development to manufacturing sites and from one manufacturing site to another) are a very effective way to ensure that all activities and deliverables are completed and that the product, service, and manufacturing processes have been adequately translated into useable specifications and procedures. Be certain that all design and development activities and deliverables are well documented and that the documentation is organized and can stand alone. That is, during an audit or inspection, your development personnel do not have to explain what all of the documents are and how they fit together and complement each other.

Treat all changes to products, services, and manufacturing processes as design changes. It is not a case of "if design controls are needed," it is a case of "how much design control is needed?" Keep in mind that all changes to design inputs (users' needs and intended uses) require design validation and some level of design verification. All changes to design outputs (products, assemblies, components, and processes) require design verification and may require design validation.

Everyone in the organization must embrace the concept that process validation is part of design transfer. Essentially, design transfer is not completed until design verification (assurance that you made the product correctly), design validation (assurance that you made the correct product) and process validation (assurance that your processes can consistently make the correct products correctly) are all successfully completed. A *validation master plan* is essential to understanding and implementing robust process validation. Process validation ensures that the right processes are in place and can be repeatedly performed to make the products your customers want and need.

The key takeaways for design control are:

- Get and keep the customers involved. Make products they want. Don't try to sell them products you made.

- Review CAPA, customer complaints, and nonconforming products as part of developing inputs.

- Treat all changes to product and processes as design changes, which therefore require some level of design control (probably minimal).

- Remember that design transfer includes design verification, design validation, and process validation.

- Link design control to your documentation and change management system.

Examples of Not-So-Good and Good Practices

ICC's marketing manager has come to the CEO with a request for a new product. The marketing manager has just learned that a major competitor is planning to launch two new products in the next year. The CEO pulls together a team and heads it. The team is charged with developing a new product that will counter the competitor's new product. The team is told it has to get this new product to the market at all costs. The team is to report to the CEO each week on progress.

The team embarks on a new product based on some improvements the marketing manager gives them. As the project progresses, team members realize that they do not have adequate financing or resources to meet the highly aggressive schedule. The CEO gives them a major pep-talk about their success being linked to the success of the company and implores them to work harder and to get what resources they can. By the time the team could hire resources for the team or to replace people who could be on the team, the market launch date will have passed.

The CEO, however, determines that ICC absolutely has to have a new product on the market; therefore the specifications and requirements are drastically cut to allow time to test prior to marketing the product. The additional features that were cut can be retrofitted in the field once they are available. ICC launches its "new" product six weeks after the competitor. The retrofit hits the field nearly three months later, requiring most of the service personnel to work double shifts to get it in place at all customers.

The aftermarket costs are higher than expected, and the number of customer complaints, reworks, and returned products are nearly 20 percent higher than for any previous product. Manufacturing problems also arise that result in back orders and scrapped products.

Meanwhile, PPI's CEO has come back from a major series of meetings held jointly with marketing and key customers. The new product development team and the PPI management team are called together and the CEO, marketing, and the two major customers present their ideas for two new products. Two new product development teams are established, with one of the key customers assigned to be part of the team. Each team puts together a development plan outlining the tasks, deliverables, and schedules.

One of the teams is making excellent progress and looks like it will meet the schedule and be on budget. The second team is struggling because its product will require the development of some revolutionary robotics to manufacture the product in adequate quantities and at acceptable costs. At a comprehensive design review, it is determined that the second team will work with the first to accelerate the release of the first product; then the combined team will tackle the second, more complicated product. The key customers are involved at sites where the new products undergo design validation.

As a result of these activities, the first product is launched two months early, and the second product is released four months later than initially planned. Both products have aftermarket costs below those previously experienced. Sales and customer responses for both products exceed the marketing plans.

Change Management and Documentation Architecture and Connections

This is where the rubber meets the road. Documentation represents the objective evidence that you have accomplished two basic requirements: (1) that you have established what you are going to do in your policies, how you are going to do these in procedures and work instructions, and (2) that you can positively demonstrate (specifically through the records and completed forms) that you have performed these policies, procedures, and work instructions correctly and adequately. It is imperative that all changes (to products, services, or processes) be documented. *There are no exceptions to this rule.*

It is also very important that people who have the right technical, quality, and management knowledge perform the review and approval of documents. This does not mean that five to 10 people need to review every document. Keep this as simple as possible. If three signatures (quality, a technical person, and the functional area involved) are adequate, then utilize that. Only add additional signatures where it is absolutely necessary and adds value. Personnel must understand the significance of their signature on a document. It means that they assume responsibility for the correctness, completeness, and accuracy of the review and/or approval of the document that they signed. It does not mean that they personally had to perform the in-depth review, but it does mean that they are responsible for ensuring that the in-depth review was performed by knowledgeable personnel.

An effective change management and documentation system should be able to have a cycle time to approve and process the change and associated documentation that does not impact the business or create a bottleneck. Good organizations can accomplish this in 24 hours. If your process is running longer than 72 hours, you are probably creating more problems than you are solving.

Similarly, the more effective and efficient change and documentation systems have a well-defined review and approval matrix. Rarely are more than three to four signatures required for approval. The usual approvers include appropriate quality assurance, technical, and management personnel. If the documentation affects multiple areas, then there may be some additional signatures. If you go above five to six signatures, you might want to rethink who is approving.

This documentation portion of the system must include provisions for:

- Architecture and format of documentation

- Documentation numbering and revision history

- Distribution of new documents and retrieval of old

- Document storage and preservation/archiving

- Record retention requirements

The documentation and change management system must include provisions for:

- Establishing an effective date

- Training prior to effective date

- Impact on design control, risk management, and validation

- Regulatory impact

- Impact on incoming, in-process, and finished goods (both in your system and in customers' possession)

Change management needs to be a comprehensive system that gathers and analyzes data regarding changes within and between products, product lines, processes, and facilities. If this sounds a lot like CAPA, that is because change management and CAPA are closely linked. Change management includes an element that looks at things like:

- How many times have you made changes for the same reason?

- How many times have you made changes to the same products or processes?

- If you made a change at one facility or product, have you made the same changes at other facilities or on other related products? If so, why? If not, why not?

As you can see, change management goes well beyond just making a change and getting it documented.

Change management and documentation apply to all areas of the quality system, not just the manufacturing documentation and process changes. All changes should be made using a risk-based approach and analysis of the impact.

Key takeaways for change management and documentation are:

- Link change management to CAPA.

- Documentation is the system that controls how fast you can make changes, because changes are not complete until they are documented.

Production and Process Control Architecture and Connections

This is the area where most regulated companies have the least amount of trouble, because requirements have been around for many years. If you are not in a regulated industry, production and process controls may be a major consideration.

The standard inclusions for the production and process control (P&PC) architecture include, at a minimum:

- Standard operating procedures, work instructions, records, and forms (including workmanship standards)

- Master production and batch records (including drawings, specifications, formulations, and so on)

- Tool, jigs, and testing equipment

- Identification, traceability, and status of components, materials, assemblies, devices, active pharmaceutical ingredients, and pharmaceutical products as they apply to your products

- Materials control (handling and storage of in-process and finished goods)

- Acceptance activities (incoming, in-process, finished product, and stability testing, including laboratory controls and reserve samples, where applicable)

- Environmental specifications, monitoring, and control

- Personal practices (health, cleanliness, and clothing)

- Packaging and labeling (including label controls)

- Calibration and maintenance

- Cleaning and disinfecting of work areas and equipment

- Rework of nonconforming product and normal reprocessing

- Handling and storage of components, materials, and products

- Handling of deviations and nonconforming components, materials, and products

This list is not all-inclusive or overly comprehensive. There are many more considerations. Remember those regulatory customers? Regulatory agencies have regulations, guidances, and compendia. Association requirements and industry standards are also readily available. Use them to make certain the list is complete and accurate for your products and markets.

The key takeaways for production and process controls are:

- Perform process risk analyses.

- Create and utilize a validation master plan.

- Link your P&PC system to change management, documentation, and CAPA.

- Treat all process changes as design changes and include design activities as necessary.

- Monitor, track, and trend P&PC data (statistical process control and other tools work well here).

Examples of Not-So-Good and Good Practices

ICC's manufacturing is headed by the CEO, who oversees all of the operations to make certain that manufacturing delivers adequate product to meet customer demand. The processes have been validated. The CEO has set up a special rework line and staffed it with some of the most experienced personnel. About 15 percent of all products need to be reworked, and of the reworked products, about 80 percent are found to be acceptable and are then packaged and shipped to customers. Additionally, ICC experiences a three percent field failure rate and has conducted two field corrective actions in the past year.

PPI has an extensive SPC program in place. Data are routinely gathered and analyzed within and between plants that manufacture the same or similar products. PPI has managed to decrease manufacturing costs by an average of four percent per year over the past three years. It has similarly been able to improve the automation based on data gathered, which has resulted in a 20 percent reduction in cycle time and a 10 percent increase in capacity. PPI has seen a steady decrease in customer complaints over the same three-year period.

Facilities, Equipment, and Utilities Architecture and Connections

The major considerations are to make certain that your facilities, equipment, and utilities are designed, constructed, and operated effectively and efficiently. To ensure this, the design should be part of the product and process development process, taking into consideration the customer requirements.

These elements need to be properly validated, so ensure that they are part of the validation master plan and have robust validations performed and documented. Revalidate as necessary. This applies most often to equipment, but utilities should be included in process risk analyses. Facilities, equipment, and utilities can have enormous impact on processes and products made from these processes.

Make certain that there are qualified personnel overseeing the facilities and utilities, especially if you have special needs, such as:

- Clean rooms or controlled environment areas with laminar flow and hepa filtration

- Specialized heating, ventilation, and air conditioning (HVAC) or humidity control

- Water systems for purified, reverse osmosis (RO), distilled (DI) and/or water for injection

- High voltage

- Electrostatic discharge, electromagnetic interference, or radio frequency (RF) isolation

- Special construction needs for heavy equipment and space for servicing equipment and facilities

Again, this is not a comprehensive list, but should get you thinking about the important considerations. Make all of the facilities, utilities, and equipment as safe and user-friendly as possible, and train everyone on their proper uses and interfaces.

Key takeaways for facilities, equipment, and utilities are:

- Make certain you identify and understand the impact of these on your processes and products.

- Have drawings and specifications for facilities and utilities.

- Include these elements in the process risk analyses.

- Make certain these elements are included in the process validation practices.

Examples of Not-So-Good and Good Practices

ICC has multiple manufacturing facilities that make the same products. The equipment and utilities have been designed and developed independently. The utilities and equipment have been put on the validation master plan for each facility and have been validated.

PPI has multiple manufacturing facilities that make the same products. The facilities have all been designed to have the same utilities and equipment. Master validation plans have been developed and executed. In addition to this, process risk analyses have been conducted and have determined that there are six key parameters that must be controlled to maximize product quality and process throughput. These parameters have been included in the SPC program.

Purchasing and Supplier Architecture and Connections

This is an element that a lot of companies figure they do well. How hard can it be to buy things and get them delivered? Placing purchase orders and documenting the requirements is the easy part. You must ensure that your requirements and specifications are communicated clearly and concisely to the suppliers, and make every reasonable attempt to ensure that they notify you in advance of changes they are preparing to make. Similarly, supplier management is a major consideration included in purchasing. This includes supplier selection, evaluation, qualification, and monitoring of performance.

The level of control (inspection and testing) performed should be risk based. Considerations for risk here include, but are not limited to:

- Criticality of the component, material, or product

- Sole versus multiple source

- Cost and lead time

- Supplier capabilities and past history

These apply to anyone who supplies products, parts, or services. Yes, contractors (contract designers, contract manufacturers, and so on), consultants, and service providers (cleaning, pest control, metrology, maintenance, and so on) should be part of the supplier management process.

It is surprising how often companies do not do supplier management well. The purchasing part usually goes pretty well; the supplier portion is usually where the issues arise.

Selecting suppliers of components, materials, and products starts in the design and development process. Suppliers should be identified at this stage and then the formal qualification process can begin thereafter.

Selection and qualification of contract manufacturers, designers, developers, and contract process developers should start at the very beginning of product or process development. Treat this like any design and development project. Start by identifying your requirements and then match them to the potential supplier capabilities and expertise. Prepare a gap analysis and perform a risk analysis for the gaps. This will help you determine if you should continue to qualify and utilize this supplier. It also provides specific information regarding information to include in the contract—and, yes, you must have a contract.

The contract should not *assume* anything, it should *assign* responsibility for everything: all activities, deliverables, responsibilities, schedules, milestones, and costs must be fully, concisely, and completely specified. It is astounding how poorly some contracts are written. Then companies wonder why the project runs over budget and over schedule.

Qualification of suppliers can be accomplished in a variety of ways—questionnaires, audits, first-article inspections. The key here is to apply the appropriate level of qualification based on the requirements versus capability, criticality, and risk analyses.

All suppliers belong on a master approved supplier listing that is reviewed, approved, and reevaluated periodically (quarterly is recommended). The periodic review is to ensure that supplier performance is acceptable. This means you need to establish criteria (metrics) that will be monitored to evaluate the performance. Some considerations for these metrics include:

- On-time delivery of components, materials, products, and services

- Purchase price variances

- Rework and retest percentages, frequency, and costs

- Number, frequency, and value of items returned to the supplier

A word about on-time delivery. I worked at a company where we implemented just-in-time (JIT) manufacturing. This requires that materials and components arrive at precisely scheduled times. A very good supplier was added to the JIT supplier list. It thought it was doing us a favor by shipping early. A shipment of heat-sensitive electronic parts arrived four days early. There was no place to store them. So on-time does not just mean that being late is the only problem. This situation was an excellent item for CAPA investigation and solution. The root cause(s) were requirements definition by the company and understanding of the requirements by the supplier.

A word of caution regarding suppliers: If you decide to grandfather suppliers, make certain you have good (that means documented) justification based on objective evidence that this is appropriate.

The key takeaways for purchasing and supplier control are:

- Make certain of a robust and comprehensive supplier management system.

- Include suppliers of all products, components, and services.

- Track and trend purchasing and supplier data and information.

Examples of Not-So-Good and Good Practices

ICC has several suppliers that it has used for many years. Many of these suppliers are sole suppliers of critical raw materials and components. Over the years, ICC has routinely had to inspect and test most of these raw materials and components. ICC does not return any unacceptable materials to the suppliers, these materials are reworked where possible or scrapped.

PPI has a comprehensive supplier management program. Suppliers are categorized based on criticality of the products or raw materials supplied, volume of materials supplied, and dollar value of the materials supplied. Part of the PPI supplier qualification process includes having representatives from the suppliers visit PPI to see where and how their parts will be utilized in PPI products. PPI has an extensive dock-to-stock program for many of its components and parts. Supplier performance is monitored monthly and reported back to suppliers. PPI has an annual supplier day where key suppliers are invited to PPI to participate in supplier performance recognition and share supplier best practices.

EVALUATE AND ALIGN THE SYSTEM

After the basic system architectures have been planned and implemented, the next step in the process is evaluating and aligning the system. This is the portion of the process where you ensure that the elements are all adequate and appropriate from a basic process and effectiveness perspective. This is also where you evaluate the links within and among the various elements to ensure that the system is wired correctly. Remember the analogy to a computer? It is not enough to have all of the parts and cables, they must be connected properly to function. It is the same with your quality system.

Many of the major problems with quality systems are the connections within and among the elements. This is where the identification of internal customer requirements plays a key role. Internal customers will help you determine not just where the connections are, but what the requirements for the connections are.

Review the figures in this chapter and make certain that you have connected all of the elements. Every element connects to every other element. This sounds a bit convoluted and complex, but, actually, it is very basic. Not always simple, but basic.

Take the time to review your policies, processes, and procedures to make certain that all of the customer requirements are included. Then evaluate the connections and linkages within and among the elements. Make certain that the various elements are connected to the others. Fundamentally, every element of the quality system has linkages to every other element. During your evaluation of the quality system, make certain that all elements have effectiveness metrics that are monitored. Ensure that all elements are included in the internal audit and management review processes.

Keep in mind that everything must feed through CAPA to management so that it can ensure that the quality system is effective. CAPA acts as the central data and information processing hub in the quality system. Each element sends data and information to the CAPA. To be effective, there must be a feedback loop to each element from CAPA. This is actually done indirectly, through management. Management analyzes the data and information, and feeds back to the elements decision information whether the priorities or resource allocations need to be changed.

Figure 4.6 depicts a very simplified linkage diagram. The diagram starts with management establishing the quality plan and translating this into goals and objectives. Each function, department, and

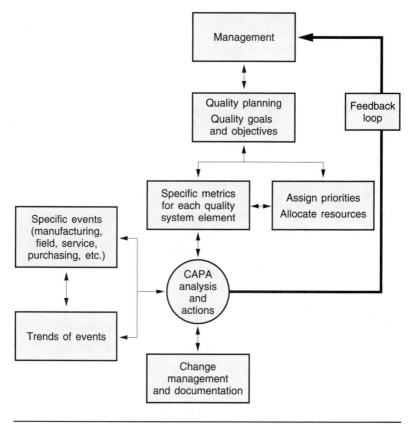

Figure 4.6 Simplified linkages in a quality system.

site translates these into specific metrics for every quality system element that applies to them. Concurrently with this process, management sets the priorities and allocates the resources discussed previously in the management architecture section.

This portion of the process is not difficult, but it can be time-consuming. Think in terms of a weekend home repair. You have just come home from work on Friday evening. You are greeted at the door by your teenagers who confess that something went wrong with the electrical outlet in the basement and now the basement electrical circuits are not working at all. To find out where the problem is, you start at the main circuit breaker box and then progressively work through the lines, junction boxes, and outlets to find out where the problem is. The evaluation of the quality system for linkages is basically the same exercise. Review each element and see if the appropriate connections are in place.

Here are some exercises to utilize:

• Pick an internal audit finding and track back the information. Is everything documented? Can you find reports communicating the finding to the appropriate functional and executive management? Is there a CAPA associated with the audit finding? Is there a root cause? I mean a *true* root cause, not just that someone didn't fill out the lab report correctly. Why did this happen? Was it due to training, discipline, attention to detail, or hiring and firing practices? Was the CAPA effective? Were there effectiveness checks and were they documented? Is there documented communication of the CAPA and results of effectiveness to the affected functional and executive management? Is there trending to see if this is part of a larger problem?

• Pick a component or material that was returned to a supplier. Go through the same basic steps just listed, including the supplier as well as the functional and executive management in the notification and feedback.

• Pick a customer complaint and perform the same basic analysis. Did you find your way back into manufacturing to fix problems? Did you find that the trail led you to design control because the issue was in the design, not the manufacturing?

A note of interest to pass on regarding customer complaints and root causes in manufacturing versus design control. For pharmaceutical companies, the vast majority (probably 85 percent or more, based on experience) of the issues from customer complaints have root causes in manufacturing. Conversely, for medical devices, the vast majority of customer complaint issues have root causes that are design related. This is one of the reasons that the FDA and ISO standards contain specific design control requirements. You must understand and address the specific nuances and requirements for your company, if you are in a regulated industry.

While you are taking some time on these exercises, do a gap analysis as part of the process. Note areas where the documentation and connections are not what they should be. The documentation and investigation should be stand-alone, self-supporting. That means that you should be able to follow the path and get all of the information needed by looking at the documentation and the documented connections, without someone having to explain it to you or lead you down the trail.

If it takes two, three, or more people to explain this to you, then there are problems with the documentation and connections. These are indications that the systems are inadequate or the connections among the elements are inadequate. Remember the basement electrical circuits? You must find the root cause and fix it. This will mean that you must correct the actual documents (in other words, the CAPA did not reference the audit report, and so on) and address the system issue of why and how this was left out of the system requirements and procedures.

When you have completed these exercises, ask other types of questions to see if the quality system is adequate in terms of architecture and implementation:

- Do specific metrics flow from the quality plan to quality goals and objectives as established by management?

- Do all of the quality system elements have adequate metrics to ensure effectiveness?

- Do the specific metrics flow into the CAPA system for evaluation, analysis, and required actions?

- Do all changes flow through change management and documentation and include evaluation for design control and regulatory impact?

- Are each of the quality system elements adequately audited throughout the year?

- Are all of the quality system elements in balance? Are they at comparable levels of architecture and maturity? (Read Chapter 5 on quality quotients to get a better feel for the specifics involved here and how to measure this.)

- Do CAPAs always include root cause analysis, effectiveness criteria, checks, and feedback to management and the affected areas?

- Are events and trends evaluated within and among products, product families, departments, and facilities?

If there are no major gaps in the exercises, and the answers to the questions are yes, then you are probably in good shape. It does not mean that you can stop and celebrate the completion of the quality system. Celebration of key accomplishments is a good idea, and it should be part of your process, but a solid, strategically planned, established, and maintained quality system means that the organization never lets up. There is a never-ending and relentless pursuit of improvement. What this means is that as part of the one-, three-, five-, and 10-year strategic quality plans, you budget investments and resources to continuously improve the quality system. Part of this budgeting process should include the ROI from previous improvements as sources of funds for subsequent improvements. It also means that as part of the quality planning process your organization reviews and refines quality goals, objectives, and associated specific metrics. Most successful companies have combined various quality tools and techniques with the quality planning process and the CAPA process to find, evaluate, and implement strategic investments to improve.

The goals here are worth repeating and include:

- Highest possible value to customers

- Highest possible quality (both in-house and in the field)

- Lowest possible costs (both for conformance and nonconformance)

- Shortest possible cycle times (for all business practices and processes)

- Lowest possible risks (safety, quality/reliability, business, and regulatory)

This is where the quality tools and techniques really come into play. They are utilized not just to identify every possible improvement and evaluate them based on risk, but to evaluate the various solutions for the best, most value-added solutions. The quality tools and techniques you apply should also allow you to identify and create synergies within and between business processes and procedures.

Creating synergies is the single most important aspect of continuous improvement. This is where the real reductions in cost, schedule, and risk are realized. That is not to say that other improvements should be forsaken—definitely not. Over the long term, however, creating synergies is the real prize.

If the solution identified does not add value, ask if it is something your organization should even think of implementing. The same holds true for quality goals, objectives, and specific metrics. Organizations have precious and limited resources; do not waste or squander them. Invest them judiciously. Do not generate data, information, paperwork, or activity unless it adds value and reduces risk.

AUTOMATE THE SYSTEM

Now comes the automation. It is listed at this point for a very specific reason. Too many times companies have jumped on the bandwagon of the latest tool or technique, investing hundreds of thousands of dollars or more, only to find that the system is not what they needed.

Automation can be accomplished concurrently with building the architecture and with evaluating and aligning the systems. A word of extreme caution here: do not attempt to automate systems until you have established some basic architecture and requirements and know what the basic business processes and procedures are going to be. You will not be able to successfully and effectively automate systems unless and until you have established the user and functional requirements and specifications. Would you go out and buy the latest and greatest car just so you could have transportation? You would start looking at your needs, your budget, and your expectations before you purchased. It is the same with automation for quality systems.

There are a lot of automated quality system tools and solutions. Remember the passage about adding value and reducing risk? This holds especially true for automation. If you get the wrong automation, it will cost more to try and get it to work and it will create more problems than it solves.

For example, your company gets the latest and greatest database manager from ACME database management systems (a purely fictitious company). It has 11 modules that can be custom-tailored to your needs (or so ACME says). If you have not yet established your needs, how will you know if this is a fit? You start to work with ACME to implement the system only to find that your data are in three different databases, none of which is directly compatible or convertible to ACME. Why didn't you know this up front? So you get a second package that will convert your data to ACME, but at what cost and delay? Next, you start a beta test to see if this automation will really work. Lo and behold, the ACME system generates 37 reports that contain detailed information on everything from documentation changes to customer inquiry response time. The problem is, your quality system is not set up to handle this type or volume of information. The reports get put into summary reports that are put into binders and given to management, who does not have the time to look at all of this information.

I used ACME company because you are to be reminded of Wile E. Coyote from the cartoons—the one who is always chasing the roadrunner. He buys the latest ACME automation; it always fails; and he always ends up buying more products in futile attempts to accomplish his goal. The results are wasted time, money, resources, and effort with no tangible return. He never catches the roadrunner.

In the ACME illustration, you have created data, information, and paperwork to what end? Is it truly value-added? Does it reduce business risks (cycle times, costs, and so on)? Does it reduce regulatory risk? No, no, and no. In fact, you may be increasing your risks because you now have information about your quality system that you should be using and are not. This can actually lead to ineffectiveness, which leads to nonconformance, which ultimately leads to increased regulatory and business risk.

This scenario illustrates why it is so important to establish the requirements first. Once you get the system working in a manual mode, or with your current automation, then get the people who will be the process owners and operators involved in establishing not just the functional requirements, but also the user requirements. Get the process owners involved with the customization and implementation of the automation. Let the process owners play with a beta test case and run it through its paces. If you find that you need to make several and/or repeated customized changes, after implementation, to get the automated systems to work or interface with your systems, that is generally an indication that you have some problems.

A real bonus here is the ability to benchmark the automation with other companies who have tried or implemented the automation. Don't just jump on the bandwagon or take the automation company's word for it. Also, consider automation from industries that may not be in your sector. If you want to see how to handle thousands of pieces of information effectively and efficiently, what industries come to mind? Do some research. Banks and financial institutions handle billions of transactions and information transfers daily. Perhaps their systems could be beneficial and adaptable. The main concept here is to think outside the box. Companies all too often get myopic in their perspective and figure that only automation and applications within their sector are worth a look.

You are going to make a substantial investment: Expect a return on the investment. If the automation company cannot provide specific information about reducing cycle time, reducing costs, and so on, then find a company that can and will provide that information.

Automation done correctly can provide some of the synergies that create real improvements. Done poorly or incompletely it becomes a black hole into which companies pour millions of dollars annually. Some areas within your quality system where automation makes sense include:

- Database and information management
- Documentation and configuration management

- Tracking and trending of CAPA, complaint, and manufacturing data

- Records retention, archiving, and retrieval

- Electronic records and signatures

- Statistical analysis, sampling plans, and statistical process control

- Design of experiments, quality function deployment, and specification setting

- Training, training requirements, and training records

There are many other areas that have automated solutions. To reiterate, make certain that you understand your real goals before automating. Ask yourself:

- Are you trying to be state-of-the-art or world-class?

- How much do you have for the initial investment?

- What is the return on your investment?

- What are the maintenance and upgrade costs?

- How often, and for how long is the system down for maintenance and upgrading?

- How long will this automation be viable and does this fit into your one-, three-, five-, and 10-year strategic quality plans?

- Do you need to have in-house technical capability or can it be outsourced and at what additional cost?

- What is the acceptable downtime?

- How will this automation improve cycle times?

- How will this automation reduce costs?

- How will this automation reduce risks?

These are all part of your requirements as well. Better to get them understood and explained at the beginning.

This all sounds so simple and basic: any manager would know this. But you would be surprised at the number of times companies do a poor job here, and it costs them tens or hundreds of thousands of dollars or more. Do the prework. Automation for the sake of automation is useless. Automation must be strategically evaluated, planned, and applied to the quality system. Get the quality system in place and know that it works, then strive to make it more effective and efficient with the automation.

CONTINUOUS IMPROVEMENT

The final phase of the quality system is the one that never ends: continuous improvement. This is where the also-rans are separated from the best-in-industry and world-class organizations. This is also an area where visionary and self-effacing management makes the difference. Management gets qualified, motivated, and self-disciplined personnel. Management can then spend its time strategically managing the system and directing, not managing the people.

The first part of continuous improvement is to identify the tools and techniques that you will apply. There are many listed previously, and there are many more than those. The important part is to pick some tools and techniques that make sense for your architecture, organization, and products (or services). And to implement a continuous improvement process as part of the CAPA system.

It is important to point out here that you do not need to use the entire tools and techniques repertoire. For example: you can use certain Six Sigma and lean tools and techniques without applying the entire tool kit and without hiring several Master Black Belts and/or Black Belts. My only caution is that you fully understand the parts of the kit you are using and also understand the limitations this might bring about.

Do not be lulled into using the tools and techniques that are the fad or that someone already knows. Do not disregard these; they may be exactly what you are looking for. Just do some homework and see what the options are and if they make sense. Remember the two basic criteria for changes and so-called improvements: (1) make certain that the changes and improvements reduce risk, and (2) make certain that they are value-added (that there is a return on the investment to external and/or internal customers).

Once you have decided on some tools and techniques, get some training and education. Determine whether you need an internal core competence in these areas or if an external source is sufficient. It may be that you need both, especially in the beginning, while you are developing your core competency in-house.

After getting your feet wet, start looking at your processes. Generally there are some low-hanging fruit that can be easily identified. Things such as a two-week documentation change cycle. Beware, though; sometimes things that look simple are not so simple. That is why the application of tools and techniques is not always enough. Do not abandon the risk-based and root-cause analyses. These are important in determining the size, scope, and complexity of the changes and projects you are contemplating.

If there are low-hanging fruit, gather them up and parade around the results. Celebrate these successes. Even though they may be small, they are the seeds from which larger things will grow. Remember that the celebration includes recognizing the process used and the people who were instrumental, and then rewarding the people who did the work. The remainder of continuous improvement requires the application of your tools and techniques to continuously evaluate and reengineer your products and processes to get them even better.

If you routinely accomplish goals for rework, scrap, and return to supplier, then raise the bar. Tighten your specifications and lower inventory level, and see what issues arise. Evaluate the required investments to make improvements and calculate the return on those investments. If you consistently have process capabilities (Cpk) greater than 1, evaluate going to 1.3 or higher.

Implement a continuous improvement process in which personnel are encouraged and empowered to make suggestions and recommendations. Put together a continuous improvement committee or group to triage these using the priority-setting tool described previously.

Keep track of the investments, the returns on the investments, and, again, celebrate, recognize, and reward success. Make the reward substantial enough to get people's attention. Reward needs to be more than recognition and praise. While these are important and help, the real returns come when you are willing to invest in continuous improvement ideas.

If you give $100 for any idea that results in savings or cost avoidance, you will get some interest and achieve limited success. How much interest and success do you think you could get if you gave a reward of three percent of the net return on the investment (total return minus the actual investment)? For example, if you invested $150,000 and saved $500,000, the net is $350,000; three percent of that is $10,500. Subtract that from the net $350,000 saved and you still have $339,500 or a net return of 226 percent. Would you be willing to make the payout? Imagine how many ideas you could get, really good ideas for only three percent. There are a lot of people who would be willing to participate, even if they had to split the three percent with a few others.

The whole idea with continuous improvement is that it takes investment to make improvement; improvements must yield respectable returns. Within one year—two maximum—you should be able to self-fund all or at least a significant portion of the continuous improvement process with the realized net returns from the previous year(s). This includes funding the capital and the resources. If you cannot get to this point, then there may be something wrong. Rethink your approach in terms of architecture, tools, techniques, and automation to get the right mix. Continuous improvement cannot be established or sustained without investment in people and systems.

Key Takeaways

- Understand the four phases.

- Determine which of these phases you are in.

- Use the information to start developing a strategic plan for the next steps in the evolution of your quality system.

ENDNOTES

1. Donald L. Kirkpatrick, *Evaluating Training Programs: The Four Levels* (San Francisco: Berrett-Koehler, 1998).
2. Frank M. Gryna, *Quality Planning and Analysis: From Product Development through Use,* 4th ed. (New York: McGraw-Hill Science/Engineering/Math, 2000).
3. Eighty-five percent capacity loading is used at two of the best-in-class companies I have worked with. Neither wanted to be quoted with this figure. Many other companies do not calculate the capacity load for individuals or functions/departments; these companies also declined ownership of the information.
4. Incredible Concepts Corporation (ICC) and Perfect Products, Inc. (PPI) are purely fictitious companies. Any resemblance to specific existing companies is purely coincidental. They represent composites, based on real-life experience from a variety of companies.
5. Bjørn Andersen and Tom Fagerhaug, *Root Cause Analysis: Simplified Tools and Techniques* (Milwaukee: ASQ Quality Press, 1999).

5

Evaluating Your Quality Quotient

This section is all about evaluating your organization and seeing where you are in terms of the four phases of quality systems. Each upcoming topic contains statements regarding your quality system. Each of the major quality system elements is given a scale range of 1 to 5; with a 1 indicating that no system exists for the specified requirement and a 5 indicating that the quality system is beyond state-of-the-art and headed toward world-class performance in the specified requirement. Your organization should review the requirements statements for each score for each quality system element. This will provide insight as to where you are and gaps versus where you want to be.

If you apply the principles outlined in this book correctly, you should significantly improve your quality quotient (Q^2) and simultaneously reduce the risks. Your quality quotient is a measure of your quality system maturity and effectiveness. Recall that risk, defined as the severity of an issue in relationship to the probability of occurrence, is the quality system's primary concern. Identifying and reducing risks are the goals of the quality system. The first part of regulatory risk is the probability of a regulatory agency finding a deficiency or nonconformance.

Keep in mind that there are no guarantees that you can have an absolute assurance that a regulatory agency will not find any issues. The second part of regulatory risk concerns the level of severity of the issues that might be found during a regulatory inspection. As with reduced probability of nonconformances, scores greater than 3 are a good indication that any issues found will not be significant.

This process is designed such that an honest and comprehensive evaluation with scores greater than 3 will greatly reduce this probability. A score of 3 or better will provide a solid set of (state-of-the-art) effective and efficient business practices and will significantly affect regulatory risk.

Again, while there are no guarantees, using the quality quotient will give you a real sense of your regulatory (and business) risks. As shown in Figure 5.1, your Q^2 and risk are inversely related: The lower your scores, the greater the risk in terms of both severity of issues and the probability that severe issues will be found. The opposite is also true: The higher your Q^2, the lower the risk. As your Q^2 increases, the probability of finding significant issues decreases and the severity of any issues identified also decreases.

Determine which number best represents the state of the quality system in your organization. It is very important that you be honest in this evaluation. Strong elements in a system will not offset weak elements. For example, having a good documentation control system does not offset a lack of well-defined quality plans and objectives.

The Q^2 scores are also an indication of how effective your quality system is. As the Q^2 exceeds 3, your cost of quality and continuous improvement efforts should start to show positive trends.

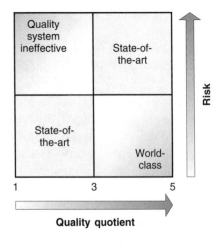

Figure 5.1   Quality quotient versus risk.

The scores you obtain give you a good indication of where your system is and can also be used for planning improvements in specific requirements. You can achieve this by reviewing the criteria for higher scores and implementing corrective actions to develop your system's elements.

The elements that are core to an effective quality system are detailed here. If you desire, you can look at the basic criteria and develop additional Q^2 criteria for any element or system you desire.

SET YOUR GOALS

Determine your goal before you start. This means evaluate if you want to be state-of-the-art or world-class. Your goals may include both. A short-term goal is state-of-the-art; a long-term goal is world-class. Make certain these are defined in your one-, three-, five-, and 10-year strategic quality plans.

It's time to get started. Start evaluating your scores and record your results in the scorecard. See Figure 5.2 for a sample Q^2 scorecard. Later in this chapter I provide criteria for each quality system element on this scorecard. Use the comments column to annotate good areas and areas for improvement. Be honest. Do not look at the levels and say, "We are basically there" or "We will be there in a few months." If you cannot provide documented, objective evidence that your organization is completely meeting all of the elements included, then go back to the next lower score.

You can and should repeat this determination of your Q^2 periodically. Your Q^2 is not like an intelligence quotient; it can and does change. This is especially true if your initial scores are less than 3. You should use the results to feed into the CAPA system where you will:

- Determine the root cause(s) at the system level.

- Develop corrective and preventive action plans (including metrics to monitor for improvement).

- Implement the plans.

- Reevaluate your Q^2.

Quality system element	Score	Comments
Management responsibility		
Corrective and preventive action		
Design control		
Change management & documentation		
Internal audit		
Training		
Process control		
Purchasing and material controls		
Inspection and testing		
Calibration and maintenance		
Control of nonconforming product		
Servicing		
Statistical techniques		

Figure 5.2 Quality quotient scorecard.

The requirements listed in each section require that procedures, work instructions, and forms are established and that specific documented objective evidence supporting the claim can be provided. Meeting the Q^2 criteria includes provisions that you have adequate numbers of trained personnel and other resources necessary to meet the criteria listed. If this is not the case, then your score should be the level at which you do have the architecture, infrastructure, and resources to implement and maintain a quality system. Again, do not be liberal here, be honest. It will help in the long run. If you give yourself too much credit, you are doing a disservice to the company. You will end up underestimating your regulatory and business risks. These will translate into increased costs and decreased effectiveness of your quality system.

Q^2 criteria can be easily incorporated into your internal audit system. It can also be utilized when evaluating suppliers.

Prepare a gap analysis sheet while you are evaluating your quality quotient. This information will be valuable and helpful in determining your course of continuous improvement.

Q² IS CUMULATIVE

The criteria listed for each score are cumulative. The requirements for a score of 3 are predicated on all of the criteria for a score of 2 being in place. If you have all of the criteria for a score of 3 and some of the criteria for a score of 4, then record a score of 3 and make some notes in the comments section regarding the additional items already in place. If you are tempted to try and play around with setting partial scores, *don't!* It will only give you a false sense of security. It is not like getting a grade point average of 3.25 or 3.5 or 3.75 as in high school or college. Here you want to be more conservative. It will help drive your continuous improvements.

Trying to determine partial scores will also dilute the effectiveness of the scores and will more than likely take more time and effort than it is worth. That is to say, it is a bad investment of time and resources. Spend that time and resources fixing or improving your quality system.

Again, there must be documented, stand-alone evidence that you have met the criteria. If it is not documented, it was not done. Each score section is a pass/fail situation. If you do not meet all of the criteria, you get the next lower score, where you have met all of the criteria.

The upcoming criteria lists are not all-inclusive. That is, they do not contain every possible criterion that could be included in each element. They are meant to provide a basic level of understanding of the requirements necessary for each score.

Keep in mind the four basic phases of the quality system: architecture and connections, evaluation and alignment, automation, and continuous improvement. Your Q² scores give you a strong indication as to which phase your quality system is in. Consider:

- Scores of 1 mean you are basically in prearchitecture and connections.

- Scores of 2 indicate architecture and connections are in place.

- Scores of 3 indicate evaluations are in place and are used for advanced alignment and effectiveness of the systems.

- Scores of 4 indicate that systems have been automated, and this information is used to ensure timeliness and effectiveness of the systems.

- Scores of 5 indicate that a proactive and customer-centric continuous improvement process is in place that encompasses the entire organization and its processes and practices.

The remainder of this chapter consists of a template to be used to develop your customized criteria. It provides a starting point and some suggestions. These are not the final criteria; they must be customized for your particular circumstances as part of the evolution of your business and quality system.

You may also find that you want to develop additional elements with associated criteria for needs specific to your business, products, or customers. For example, if you provide services and products, you may want to include an additional element specifically concerning the types of services you provide and create the associated criteria for scores of 1 through 5 based on the requirements listed and using the examples as a starting point.

Keep in mind as you determine your Q^2 that it is a snapshot in time of where you are. If you are a start-up or a turnaround, your Q^2 score can and should change. That is why it is important to determine your score periodically, that is also why it is a good practice to tie your Q^2 score in with your internal auditing process. You can also use the Q^2 score concept when evaluating acquisitions and suppliers. So let's get into the actual criteria sorted by quality system element.

MANAGEMENT RESPONSIBILITY CRITERIA

1. Management has not established a formal quality organization and has not established a formal quality plan or measurable objectives.

2. A quality organization exists and controls quality using inspections. A quality culture is starting to emerge. Authority and responsibility for quality is defined, including quality assurance and quality control. Requirements for quality policy, plan, and objectives are defined. Many functions have quality plans. Requirements exist for management reviews, and a management representative has been assigned. The basics of a CAPA system are in place, and use of quality measurements is becoming consistent.

3. Senior management has documented policy, plan, objectives (including measurable metrics), responsibility, and authority for all elements of the quality system. Requirements for management reviews of the quality system are documented. Quality objectives and metrics are consistently used by all functions in the organization. Management communicates the quality policy and vision to all employees. Effectiveness of the quality system is routinely and specifically measured, monitored, and reviewed by management. Evidence of quality improvements exists. Quality plans are fully integrated into the annual planning process with appropriate objectives, metrics, and resources to ensure that quality plans achieve the expected results. Management utilizes CAPA as the core monitoring system. Measures and rewards are becoming linked to quality improvement. Management reviews, CAPA, and internal audits are linked.

4. Quality plans exists for all functions and are based on customer (both external and internal) requirements. Quality vision, plan, policy, and objectives are well communicated to all employees. Quality planning incorporates both external and internal customer requirements, benchmarking of best-in-class, and supplier performance. Quality system metrics and measures are used to monitor the effectiveness of the quality system and, when appropriate, implement corrective and preventive action. Senior management is visibly and actively involved in oversight and directing quality. The organization is utilizing a risk-based approach to continuously improving the quality planning process and quality system effectiveness. Proactive quality planning is effectively used to drive the organization to higher levels of performance. Employee development and reward systems are linked to meeting quality requirements. Strategic quality planning for one-, three-, five-, and 10-year periods is in

place, and measures are effectively used to improve core business processes. Management effectively prioritizes projects and assigns appropriate resources.

5. Executive and functional management use the quality planning, objectives, and deployment processes to continuously measure and improve core business practices. All employee activities in the organization are linked to quality plans and objectives. Continuous quality improvement is a normal business practice, which includes active management involvement. Meeting external and internal customer requirements is clearly demonstrated with activities, objectives, and metrics, including customer satisfaction. Company vision and mission are established with world-class performance as the objective. The entire organization works synergistically to develop and manufacture products and to provide services that exceed customer requirements. The entire organization, led by management's example, proactively utilizes quality planning, objectives and specific metrics, and CAPA in conjunction with quality tools, techniques, and automation to consistently identify and reduce safety, regulatory, quality, reliability, and business risks. Return on quality investments is routinely measured and monitored.

CAPA CRITERIA

1. No system exists to ensure implementation of effective corrective and preventive actions that can identify and eliminate the root cause(s) of actual and potential nonconformance of product and service.

2. An informal or partial system exists. The focus is mainly reactive and primarily concerns manufacturing issues and corrective action. In-process failures and returned products are not always analyzed to determine the root cause(s) of failure. Requirements and responsibilities for corrective actions are defined and documented.

3. A more complete system is evident. Reactive requirements for corrective and preventive action are documented and defined. Effectiveness metrics are used to ensure adequacy of CAPA. Complete

records are available and cross-reference applicable support documentation (in other words, master and batch records, risk analyses, root cause analyses, verifications, and validations). Responsibilities for implementation of CAPA activities are defined and documented. Analysis of deviations and nonconformance are available in most production and related areas. Most corrective actions are monitored for completion. Focus on preventive actions is becoming evident. CAPA includes input of quality data from all quality system elements. CAPA captures management review action items, internal audit inputs, and tracks and trends quality data.

4. The system is fully implemented. The system ensures that evaluation and analysis results and corrective/preventive actions are documented. Effectiveness of the system is evaluated and reviewed by appropriate management for corrections, corrective actions, and preventive actions. Employees are adequately trained, and documentation of training is evident. Trending systems are used to analyze all sources of quality data. Root cause analyses are robust and documented. The scope of the CAPA system is clearly defined to include monitoring of all specific metrics and quality system elements in the facility. The CAPA system is collecting and analyzing customer satisfaction data and information. In-depth root cause analyses are undertaken to include all aspects of the business practices and processes. Employees are empowered, knowledgeable, and proactively using the system. The corrective/preventive action system utilizes effective measures to ensure that root causes of nonconformances are identified and eliminated. A wide set of quality metrics and data are tracked and trended within and between products, functions, and, where applicable, sites. Root causes for systemic issues are aggressively pursued. Effective feedback loops are established and true systemic root causes are being identified and resolved. All CAPAs have short- and long-term effectiveness checks. The CAPA system has been automated to provide faster CAPA cycle times and better data gathering and analysis.

5. Focus of CAPA is prevention. A major focus of the CAPA system is continuous improvement and returns justify investments. Closed-loop systems provide immediate feedback and resolution of issues. Quality planning includes objectives and metrics for reducing

product and process nonconformance. Metrics show continuous progress in all functional areas and include focus on customer satisfaction. Advanced statistical techniques are used to identify worst-case conditions that could lead to nonconformance. The root cause analyses are used in all functional areas of the business. Effectiveness measures are evident and used throughout the organization to drive continuous improvement. The CAPA system is fully deployed and focuses on timely and effective analysis and nonconformance reduction for all products, services, and internal business processes. The CAPA system also includes gathering and evaluating noncomplaint customer information and data. Advanced quality tools and techniques are applied to CAPA projects. Measures are linked to customer satisfaction goals. CAPA data are used to develop quality plans, objectives, and metrics.

DESIGN CONTROL CRITERIA

1. No formal system exists for product and process development.

2. An informal design control system exists. The design control requirements are generally known, with design activities selected on a project-by-project basis. Phase reviews are occasionally and informally held. A system is implemented with most of the required steps documented. Employee training requirements are defined. Design reviews tend to focus on project status rather than design quality.

3. The design control system is fully defined. Customer requirements are used to define new product specifications and designs. Design and development plans and procedures drive development. Required records are available and stand-alone. Design and phase reviews are conducted at specified intervals, documented, and focus on evaluating the technical and quality aspects of the design, the use of the design and development plan and design control procedures, as well as cost and schedule. Customer complaints and CAPA are integral parts of concurrent product and process development. Traceability within and between design inputs, outputs, verifications, and validations is evident. Basic risk analysis tools are used throughout the product lifecycle. Quality tools and techniques (in other words, design of experiments, quality function deployment,

and response surface mapping) are utilized in design verification, design validation, and process validation activities.

4. The design control system is fully implemented, with processes that include provisions for planning, customer requirements, inputs, phased reviews, outputs, verification and validation, transfer, changes, and documentation. Records and documents of successful completion of activities per the design and development plan are well organized and accessible in the design history files. More advanced quality tools such as failure mode and effects analysis (FMEA), analysis of variance (ANOVA), and design of experiments (DOE) are used. Development cost and cycle time are evaluated and reviewed by appropriate management personnel. The design process effectively considers human factors, manufacturability, and serviceability requirements. Where applicable, analyses and testing are based on statistically sound rationale. Development cycle times, budgets, and resource utilization are tracked and monitored. Customers are included and integrated into the development process and new products and services surpass customer requirements. Aftermarket costs are used to evaluate design effectiveness.

5. Customer and supplier involvement in the design process is well documented. Design requirements are derived from sources including current production issues, field returns, customer complaints, and service records. Techniques such as quality function deployment (QFD) and Six Sigma are used to establish and fully understand customer requirements. Automation and innovation drive design process improvement; effective measures are evident. Statistical techniques are being used to analyze and identify issues and potential problems that can be proactively resolved. The product development process has been optimized to ensure that customer requirements drive products in an effective and efficient manner. The development system is fully deployed, utilizing inputs from all functional groups to continuously and proactively identify external and internal customer needs, satisfy business goals and objectives, and incorporate customer needs, wants, and requirements into world-class products. Customer satisfaction measures show that products continuously exceed customer requirements. Post-launch meetings are used to evaluate performance of the products and the strengths and weaknesses of the design control process.

CHANGE MANAGEMENT AND DOCUMENTATION CRITERIA

1. No formal system exists for the identification and control of change, including associated documentation, data, and records.

2. Individual functions/departments utilize their own approach to change control, records, documentation, and data control. Requirements for a centralized change- and document-control department are not well defined. A formal system is becoming evident and it is partially implemented. No definitive review or approval requirements for documentation have been established. Minimal system effectiveness measures have been implemented.

3. The change management and documentation elements are well defined and integrated. Responsibilities for implementation and maintenance of a centralized system are defined and documented. All quality system changes are managed through a coordinated system. Design and regulatory impact are documented for all changes; criteria for verification and validation needed to support changes are defined and implemented. Controls are evident for documents, data, and records. System effectiveness is measured and reviewed by appropriate management personnel. Defined review and approval matrices have been established. Record retention, archival, dissemination, and retrieval practices have been established. Changes include impact analysis for regulatory, quality, validation, risk, design, and manufacturing. All changes and associated records, documentation, and data are maintained to ensure availability and legibility.

4. Changes and associated records, documents, and data are being managed and monitored by effectiveness measures. All quality system records, plans, reports, and files are complete and stand-alone. All changes are communicated to the appropriate people. All changes are reviewed and approved by applicable management, technical staff, and quality personnel. Required verifications and validations are completed prior to the implementation of changes. The system utilizes feedback from all functional areas to drive continuous improvement. Systems are focused on preventing documentation errors and

improving accuracy and efficiency. Quality tools, techniques, and automation are utilized to continuously reduce change cycle times, records management, and configuration management. Change management includes use of statistical tools for tracking and trending of changes. Where applicable, validated electronic records and signatures systems are utilized.

5. Quality planning is used to define and drive change management and document improvement goals. Where possible, the human element has been designed out of the process to reduce clerical and typographical errors. Measures for effectiveness, including cycle time, are visible and drive improvement. Changes and their associated and required documents and records are complete, accurate, and readily available and cross-reference all other CAPA-associated documentation and information. The change-control process is timely and effective, as based on specific quality plan objectives and metrics. All changes are tracked and trended for their impact on the entire business and associated business practices. Continuous improvements are based on customer impact and value-added criteria and are tracked through the CAPA system for timeliness and effectiveness.

INTERNAL AUDIT CRITERIA

1. No formal system exists to ensure that audits are scheduled, conducted, and followed up to determine the effectiveness of the quality system and its compliance to established requirements.

2. An informal or partial audit system exists. Application is dependent on individuals. Formal audit criteria and checklists are not documented. Audit results are reported, but limited in scope or requirements. Training requirements are defined. An audit schedule is documented.

3. A complete audit system is fully implemented. An audit schedule exists and is reviewed and updated. Requirements and procedures are documented and well defined. Audit effectiveness metrics have been established. Follow-up and audit closure is evident. Audit training has been initiated. All auditors have adequate training

and experience. The auditors are independent of audited areas and are adequately trained, with documented training records. Reports are reviewed by appropriate levels of management. Audit checklists are updated annually. Audit planning includes all functional areas (system elements). Responsibilities for implementation are defined and documented. All of the elements of the quality system are audited at least once per year with additional follow-up where indicated. Audits include assessment activities.

4. Follow-up corrective and preventive action and audit closure is evident. Schedules are being followed, with documented rationale for changes. Effectiveness of the system is being evaluated and reviewed by appropriate management personnel. The audit system focuses on the quality system's effectiveness as well as its compliance to regulatory requirements. Audits are perceived as a value-added activity. The internal process and results are reviewed periodically to improve compliance and the system. Formal checklists and criteria are utilized for audits, and these are reviewed and updated as part of each annual audit cycle. Auditing includes compliance and effectiveness of business unit systems. Audit issues are captured in the CAPA system. Audit results are tracked and trended within and between products, product lines, and department systemic issues. Audits and assessment results are used to identify continuous improvement opportunities.

5. Quality auditing is based on regulatory customer requirements; quality plans, objectives, and metrics; and internal customers' requirements. Audit results are used to drive continuous improvement of the effectiveness of internal audits. Audit resources from outside the facility are used to provide added objectivity and flexibility. Auditing includes installation and service, reviewing customer survey efforts, evaluation of effectiveness of continuous improvement, ability to provide customer inputs into designs, benchmarking, and management controls. Continuous improvement is ensured through self-audits performed by empowered employees who proactively identify issues and resolve them. Auditing and assessment is extensively used as a management tool and is a recognized influence in quality management system development and improvement.

TRAINING CRITERIA

1. No formal training of personnel is performed.

2. An informal or partial training system exists primarily for production personnel. Records are incomplete. Requirements and responsibilities are known on a general level. Training is focused on skills with limited focus on employee development.

3. Training requirements, schedules, and records exist for production and related functions; compliance to schedules and requirements is monitored. All functions and departments, including management, have documented training requirements. Training system effectiveness measures have been initiated. Training includes quality system, regulatory requirements, product and business orientation, safety, and job-specific elements. Responsibility for training is defined. All functions have documented training requirements. Training requirements are based on job/function descriptions, and all personnel have the appropriate education, training, and experience to perform their functions. All training has effectiveness checks. All trainers have documented qualifications. Retraining requirements have been established.

4. A fully functional training system is implemented. The system is implemented throughout the facility/organization using means such as a training matrix to identify core and elective training requirements for all employees, including management. Employees are trained on quality tools, techniques, and automation; training records are maintained. Compliance to training requirements is measured and monitored by management personnel. Training requirements are included in quality planning as a means of improving employee effectiveness and productivity. Training includes awareness/knowledge training, competency, and proficiency training where these are needed to ensure effective performance of functions. A training matrix is designed to ensure that all employees have the necessary skills to be proficient in their jobs and have educational opportunities to enhance utilization and development. The training system has been automated to ensure that training is identified, conducted, and documented. Post-training criteria, including rework,

scrap, retest, nonconformances, and deviations, are used to monitor training effectiveness.

5. Management routinely reviews the training matrices to ensure that the training program provides adequate and timely training for all employees (including management) and an opportunity to excel in their position. Measurements of training effectiveness and success exist. Training is actively used as a method to develop a skilled, knowledgeable, and highly efficient workforce that can meet the challenge of the business mission. Training results (effectiveness check measurements) demonstrate that employees have the skills to fully satisfy customers with world-class products and services. Training is openly encouraged to ensure employee development. Training allowances for external training are established. Minimum time and budget amounts are budgeted annually for employee training.

PRODUCTION AND PROCESS CONTROL CRITERIA

1. No formal process control system exists. Written procedures do not exist for all operations, process monitoring, and control elements. This includes laboratory, environmental monitoring, cleaning, manufacturing (assembly, test, and inspection), packaging, labeling, product identification and traceability, handling, storage, and distribution.

2. A partial system exists with some written procedures. Process control requirements are generally known. Work instructions are incorporating adequate requirements for process monitoring and control. Maintenance of the production area and of processing equipment is partially defined and implemented. All manufacturing and packaging processes have been qualified. Responsibilities for implementation of process controls have been defined and documented. Production training requirements are defined and implemented. Environmental requirements have been defined and are monitored.

3. All processes affecting product quality have been identified, documented, validated where appropriate, and controlled through a

formal validation master plan. All processes have been mapped or flowcharted for process-risk analyses. Definition and validation of all special processes is complete, including monitoring required for special processes. All production (assembly, test, and inspection) software has been adequately validated. Statistical techniques, including statistical process control (SPC), are used to analyze data from qualifications and validations. Effectiveness measures of the process control system have been initiated. Equipment maintenance programs are fully implemented. The process control system is fully implemented. Special processes are validated using a clearly defined protocol. All employees are adequately trained, and training records are available. Effectiveness of the system is measured and reviewed by appropriate management. Records of qualifications, validations, and process monitors are documented and maintained. Statistical techniques are used to analyze data for trends. Workmanship standards are being effectively used. Deviations and nonconformances are tracked, trended, and fed into the CAPA system.

4. Process controls are focused on prevention, not detection. Statistical techniques such as DOE, response surface mapping, and SPC are used. Production, inspection, and quality software are controlled and regularly verified for proper operation and revision. Customer feedback and field performance data are factored into corrective actions. Process control improvements are being factored into quality planning. Process parameters are clearly monitored and controlled. Quality objectives include customer-centric metrics for manufacturing cycle times and value to the customer. In-process/final inspection yields are high, predictable, and improving. Techniques such as Six Sigma, lean manufacturing, or QFD are used to identify and implement customer requirements for process control improvements. Quality tools, techniques, and automation are utilized to track and trend process control problems and issues.

5. There is evidence of continuous improvement, driven by quality plans and objectives. Increasing inventory turns are evident. Systems (using statistical techniques) are being used in conjunction with automated monitoring and feedback resulting in proactive identification, analysis, and resolution of issues and potential problems that improve customer satisfaction. Measurement systems are in place to monitor customer satisfaction. Manufacturing systems and

controls are designed to be error-free and cost-effective. Rework, scrap, cycle times and throughputs are all showing continuous improvements. Customer satisfaction measures show that the facility is consistently delivering goods and services that exceed customer requirements. There is a closed-loop feedback system driving continuous improvement.

PURCHASING AND MATERIAL CONTROL CRITERIA

1. No formal system exists to ensure that only raw materials, components, manufacturing materials, subassemblies, and finished products that meet specified requirements are used, processed, or distributed.

2. Functional areas approach purchasing and material control independently and differently. Purchasing and material control is performed. Departmental or functional procedures are defined or documented. Partial inspection records exist. Responsibilities for purchasing and material control are defined and documented. Effectiveness measures have been initiated. Purchasing and material control records are incomplete. Supplier/user feedback has been initiated. Statistical techniques are used in some areas. Basic procedures for receiving, incoming, in-process, finished goods, and distribution are in place.

3. Purchasing and material control procedures include selection, qualification, and monitoring of suppliers and materials. Required records are available. The system's effectiveness is measured, and results are reviewed by appropriate management personnel. All suppliers are on an approved supplier listing. The transition from a reactive quality control–based system to a proactive quality assurance–based system (proactive supplier selection, qualification, and monitoring) is beginning. CAPA is utilized as an integral part of purchasing and material control discrepancies, deviations, and nonconforming materials. Purchasing and supplier performance data are tracked and trended. Employees are adequately trained, and documentation of training is evident. Formal procedures for purchasing, receiving, handling, and storage of materials are in place.

4. Purchasing and material control activities and results are effectively managed through the CAPA system and management reviews. Positive linkage exists between purchasing, quality assurance, and suppliers, resulting in timely resolution of material and product issues. Supplier and internal customer feedback and field-performance data are factored into corrective actions. The transition to a proactive quality assurance–based system is complete. All employees understand quality requirements; self-inspection is widely utilized before sending product to the next operation. Supplier performance and purchasing and material control effectiveness are high, predictable, and improving. Quality tools, techniques, and automation are leveraged to improve effectiveness and efficiency. Suppliers are routinely integrated into the specifications development process.

5. Empowered employees have fully integrated purchasing and material control goals into the quality and manufacturing processes. Supplier and internal customer feedback are utilized in identifying and eliminating potential issues. The transition to an assurance-based system is complete. Purchasing and material control are moved as far upstream as possible. Where appropriate, self-inspection; parametric release; skip-lot; and supplier, purchasing, and material control are in use. Advanced statistical techniques are being used to analyze, identify, and eliminate issues and potential problems. Systems are designed with optimum inspection that provides the highest confidence that all products will meet requirements. Customer feedback on performance of products and distribution are utilized to drive additional improvements.

INSPECTION AND TESTING CRITERIA

1. No formal system exists to ensure that only raw materials, components, manufacturing materials, subassemblies, and finished products that meet specified requirements are used, processed, or distributed.

2. Functional areas approach inspection and testing independently and differently. Inspection and testing is performed. Departmental or functional procedures are defined or documented. Partial

inspection records exist. Responsibilities for inspection and testing are defined and documented. Effectiveness measures have been initiated. Inspection and testing records are incomplete. Supplier/user feedback has been initiated. Statistical techniques are used in some areas. Basic procedures for receiving, incoming, in-process, finished goods, and distribution are in place.

3. Inspection and testing procedures include statistically valid sampling plans and statistical method rationale. Required records are available. The system's effectiveness is measured, and results are reviewed by appropriate management personnel. The transition from a reactive quality control–based system to a proactive quality assurance–based system (designing quality into products and processes and designing out the need for non-value-added inspection) exists. CAPA is utilized as an integral part of inspection and testing discrepancies, deviations, and nonconforming materials. Employees are adequately trained, and documentation of training is evident. All equipment is calibrated and maintained according to procedures. Formal procedures for receiving, incoming, in-process, finished goods, and distribution are in place.

4. Inspection and testing activities and results are effectively managed. Positive linkage exists between final inspection, in-process inspection, receiving inspection, engineering, and suppliers resulting in timely resolution of material and product issues. Results are routinely tracked and trended in the CAPA system for effectiveness and potential improvements. Analytical testing methods have been validated and experimental error is known. Comparative references and testing software are controlled and regularly verified for accurate operation and revision. Supplier/user feedback and field-performance data are factored into corrective actions. The transition to a proactive quality assurance–based system is almost complete. All employees understand quality requirements; self-inspection is widely utilized before sending product to the next operation. Receiving, incoming inspection, in-process inspection, and final inspection are showing effectiveness, acceptance is high, and results are predictable and improving. Quality tools, techniques, and automation are leveraged to improve effectiveness and efficiency. Mean time to and between failures, back order rates, and other customer perception of quality metrics are used.

5. Empowered employees have fully integrated inspection and testing goals into the quality and manufacturing processes. Supplier/user feedback is utilized in identifying and eliminating potential issues. The transition to an assurance-based system is complete. Inspection and testing are moved as far upstream as possible. Where appropriate, self-inspection, parametric release, skip-lot, and supplier inspection and testing are in use. Advanced statistical techniques are being used to analyze, identify, and eliminate issues and potential problems. Systems are designed with optimum inspection that provides the highest confidence that all products will meet requirements. Customer feedback on performance of products and distribution is utilized to drive additional improvements.

CALIBRATION AND MAINTENANCE CRITERIA

1. No formal system exists to control, calibrate, and maintain inspection, measuring, test, and manufacturing equipment used to demonstrate a product's conformance to requirements.

2. A formal system exists. Requirements and responsibilities are established. Not all equipment and standards are traceable to recognized national standards. Procedures are at least partially documented. Calibration standards are traceable to national standards. The system and supporting procedures are defined, documented, and partially implemented in all areas of the facility. Comparative references (for example, gold standard) and test software used in production/inspection are identified and controlled. Training requirements have been defined and training has been started.

3. Evidence shows that the system is implemented in production and inspection areas. System effectiveness measures have been initiated. Users of calibrated equipment are aware of their responsibilities with respect to maintaining calibrated equipment. Calibration equipment and maintenance requirements (including software and gold standards) are documented. Comparative references are controlled and periodically checked for proper operation and revision. The system requires notification of out-of-calibration equipment. All equipment is identified and labeled, and the calibration status is

documented and maintained. Calibration and maintenance issues are captured in the CAPA system.

4. The system is fully implemented in all areas that use measuring, inspection, or test equipment. Responsibilities for implementation are defined and documented. Employees are adequately trained, and documentation of training is evident. System effectiveness is evaluated and reviewed by appropriate management personnel. Adequate records are maintained including appropriate disposition of product manufactured or inspected with out-of-calibration equipment. Contracted services are regularly audited. Data are recorded and used to predict equipment performance. Statistical methods are used to determine calibration and maintenance intervals. Comparative references and test software are controlled and regularly verified for proper operation and revision. Calibration intervals are periodically reviewed and adjusted as needed. The system includes tracking and trending information of effective measurements designed to identify opportunities for improvement. The recall system ensures that equipment is always submitted for calibration and maintenance on time. Quality tools, techniques (in other words, gauge repeatability and reproducibility), and automation are utilized to ensure calibration schedules and status. The CAPA system is utilized for out-of-calibration issues.

5. Effective quality planning drives system improvements goals. Continuous improvements of the system are evident. Employees are empowered to identify and initiate improvements. Continuous improvement is built into the system. Issues and potential problems are identified and resolved proactively by empowered personnel. There are no measurement errors associated with inaccurate equipment or suspect calibrations. Equipment location data are accurate. Calibration and maintenance turnaround is timely. Unplanned down and lost time is minimal to nonexistent.

CONTROL OF NONCONFORMING PRODUCT CRITERIA

1. No formal system exists to ensure identification, segregation, investigation, documentation, and appropriate disposition of

nonconforming raw materials, components, manufacturing materials, subassemblies, and products.

2. A system exists. Requirements and responsibilities are generally known. The system depends upon individual initiatives. Documented procedures for some nonconformance situations exist. The system to control nonconforming product is implemented in some areas of the facility.

3. The documented system includes all functional areas where nonconforming items can be found. Appropriate disposition rationale is documented and evident. Effectiveness measures have been initiated. Employees are adequately trained, and documentation of training is evident. Traceability of nonconformance is documented. Effectiveness of the system is measured and reviewed by appropriate management personnel. The CAPA system is used to drive corrective and preventive action on all dispositions of nonconforming products. Nonconforming raw materials, components, and products are routinely returned to suppliers. SPC and other tools and techniques are used to track and trend process parameters as they relate to product nonconformances.

4. The focus of CAPA in production has shifted to prevention. Improvement goals have been established to reduce root causes of nonconformance. Effective trending systems have been developed and implemented. Quality planning includes goals for reducing nonconformance. There is evidence of improvement in all functional areas. Advanced statistical techniques are used to identify worst-case conditions that could lead to nonconformance. Measurements are visible and closely tied to organizational goals such as cost savings and waste reduction. Quality tools, techniques, and automation are utilized to improve effectiveness of tracking, trending, and resolving nonconforming product issues. Internal nonconforming product and field performance are correlated by linking the CAPA, customer complaint, and nonconforming product systems and data.

5. Nonconformances and resulting reprocessing or rework are minimal and are automatically tracked and linked to appropriate corrective and preventive actions. More sophisticated statistical tools and techniques (Taguchi methods, Six Sigma, and cost of quality) are routinely used to identify and improve processes and products.

The system provides quick segregation and analysis of nonconforming products, including notification of all involved functions. Statistical techniques are being used to analyze and identify issues and potential problems that can be resolved proactively. Closed-loop systems ensure continuous, proactive improvement. Scrap and rework is minimal and predictable. Measurements show consistently low levels of nonconforming items. Continuous improvements are based on value to the customer.

SERVICING AND INSTALLATION CRITERIA

1. There is no evidence of a systematic process to analyze and service products.

2. Returned products are repaired with an informal servicing and installation system. Adequate repairs are dependent on individuals. Servicing and installation of products is partially documented. Methods are partially documented and data are collected. Records are maintained. The system is partially implemented. Servicing and installation records are linked to the device history records. Servicing and installation procedures exist. Training requirements exist.

3. The servicing and installation system is fully implemented, and service personnel are appropriately trained. Training records are maintained. Special processes are validated. Disciplined diagnostic, servicing, and installation methods are generally used. Initial effectiveness measures have been implemented. Service and installation records are reviewed for complaints and tracked and trended in the CAPA system. Service and installation issues are captured and evaluated in the CAPA system. New designs consider input and data from returned products and servicing.

4. Service results, including on-site service, are reviewed for reportable events, and data are analyzed for trends requiring corrective action in manufacturing or design. Procedures ensure that serviced/repaired products meet requirements as specified in design requirements. Effectiveness measures are well-established and effectively used to improve product and servicing and installation

performance. Effective corrective-action systems are implemented and monitored to ensure that corrective actions have resolved issues causing service-related problems. Trending analysis of data is well established. Quality tools, techniques, and automation are utilized to improve effectiveness of servicing and installation and service records. Servicing and installation results are compared to the mean time to and between failure rates and product risk analyses.

5. Servicing and installation and return data, including customer satisfaction data, are routinely reviewed, analyzed, and included in the development of new products. Servicing and installation goals are included in quality planning and new product development. Employees are using measurements, including customer surveys, to drive system improvements. Servicing and installation and return procedures are continuously analyzed and measured to identify improvements that will enhance customer service/satisfaction. Service and warranty costs are tracked and trended and are demonstrating continuous improvement. Customer satisfaction surveys show that service and installation consistently exceeds requirements.

STATISTICAL TECHNIQUES CRITERIA

1. The use of statistical techniques and sampling plans is isolated or inadequate so that no conclusions can be drawn. No systematic approach exists.

2. A formal system is evident and is partially implemented. Implementation is not uniform throughout all areas. Procedures are documented for appropriate use of statistical techniques in production and quality functions. Some statistical applications are a regular part of business decision making.

3. A well-established system exists. Responsibilities for implementation are defined and documented. Initial effectiveness measures of the system are evident. Statistical tools and sampling plans are actively used in many functions. All sampling plans are documented and based on accepted standards or methods. All methods utilized for comparative or analytical statistics have documented justification. Statistical training is included in the training matrix.

4. The system is fully implemented, with effective procedures that require statistical techniques and sampling plans to be used in such a manner that appropriate data are collected, evaluated, and reported. The entire quality system effectiveness is evaluated using appropriate statistical techniques and reviewed by appropriate functional and executive management. All validation and verification activities utilize adequate sampling plans and statistical methods. Personnel are adequately trained, and documentation of training is evident. Quality tools, techniques, and automation are routinely utilized to improve effectiveness of sampling plans and statistical analyses.

5. Applications of statistical techniques are required in the quality planning process. Employees are knowledgeable and effectively use statistical tools and sampling plans. Use of these tools and plans is evident in all parts of the quality system. Statistical tools such as Six Sigma, SPC and DOE, lean manufacturing, and balanced scorecards are widely used to understand customer requirements and to develop products and services that are proven to consistently meet customer requirements. Evidence of statistical tools that analyze and identify issues and potential problems that can be resolved proactively can be seen throughout the facility. Systems and processes are predictable, in control, and continually measured by empowered and knowledgeable employees. The use of statistical tools and techniques is evident throughout the company.

UNDERSTANDING YOUR QUALITY QUOTIENT

Based on the scores that you get, you will need to develop a plan to bridge the gaps. If your scores are 1 and 2, then you need to focus on building the architecture of your quality system. Get the system formalized and start integrating it into your daily way of doing business.

If your scores are 2 and 3, then you need to focus on refining the systems in place and aligning them to create quality system synergies. If your scores are 3 and 4 then you are definitely on the right track. You should start considering automation as a means to enhance the performance of your quality system. If your scores are 4 and 5, then you are doing very well. Continue to drive your quality system toward even higher levels of effectiveness and efficiency.

If your scores are all over the board, then you need to focus on aligning your systems. First, do a root cause analysis to determine why you have so much discrepancy. Then get all of the systems to the same basic level. Once this has been accomplished, move them to the next level(s). A wide variation in scores (more than one point from the average) indicates your system has some weak links that need to be fixed.

The urgency associated with getting all of the elements at the same level depends on two things: what are the regulatory and business risks associated with your scores? And where is your organization in terms of business lifecycles?

If your goal is to be state-of-the-art, then all of your scores should be 3. If your goal is to be world-class, then your scores should be 4s and 5s. If you are still on your journey to being world-class, then your scores could be 3s, but you should have a gap analysis and detailed plans documenting the activities, deliverables, roles and responsibilities, and time frames for completing the process.

Key Takeaways

- Understand the quality quotient criteria.

- Determine your quality quotient.

- Use the scores to develop your strategic plans for improving your quality system.

6

The Roles and Core Competencies in a Strategic Quality System

The roles that the various groups, departments, or functions within the organization play in establishing and maintaining a strategically viable quality system must be defined by executive management. Management must similarly determine if the core competencies used to accomplish these functions should be part of the infrastructure or outsourced. These decisions are made, as are all decisions regarding the quality system, based on risk. Here it is not the traditional risk analysis, but a risk/benefit analysis. This is done to determine the best fit in terms of logistics, costs, and capabilities in the short term and the longer term. This means management must have a basic road map for the quality system in the short and long terms.

This chapter will deal with the skills required for the quality system. The focus here is on the skills required to establish, maintain, and continuously improve the quality system. These skills are standard for any quality system. There are obviously many skills that will not be mentioned here. The main skills and responsibilities included are for those in the following roles:

- Executive management

- Functional/departmental management

- Management representative

- Quality assurance/quality control functions

These are functions that require internal core competencies to establish and maintain a strategic quality system. Other core competencies may be outsourced based on risk (business and regulatory).

All roles in a successful strategic quality system require commitment and communication. Everyone working within a strategic quality system must be committed to making the system work and to continuously improving it.

Experience has shown that in many organizations, knowledge and information are considered power, and many people like to gather power and leverage it for personal or departmental gain. *This has to be changed.* It leads to the silo effect, which perpetuates the practice of information hoarding. This, of course, is diametrically the opposite of what a strategic quality system is there to accomplish.

A strategic quality system is open to sharing, without blame or guilt, for the good of the organization. This does not mean that there is no discipline or accountability. It simply means that there are no witch hunts and inquisitions. This is why open and honest communication and genuine commitment to the organization through the quality system are so important. Everyone in the organization must know what information and data need to be gathered and communicated and how to do this.

Functions and responsibilities other than the specific four listed that have quality system implications are also included with some of the basic requirements defined. These functions and responsibilities may be partially or totally outsourced, where risk-based analysis deems it appropriate.

EXECUTIVE MANAGEMENT

The strategic quality system is top-down in terms of commitment, understanding, and oversight orientation. Therefore, executive management must have not only an awareness of, but a thorough understanding of all elements and requirements involved in establishing and maintaining the quality system. This means that, in addition to their MBAs and experience with sales, finance, accounting, and marketing, executive management must also have a keen understanding of:

- The customers' (both internal and external) requirements

- All applicable regulatory, association, and industry standards and requirements where the company's products and services are provided

- Each element within the quality system, how it works and how the systems are integrated/connected

- The specifics regarding the implementation of management responsibilities, CAPA, and continuous improvement tools and techniques

Executive management has two basic functions. The first is to establish the priorities for the entire organization utilizing a risk-based approach. This includes establishing quality planning (short- and long-term), objectives, and the associated metrics, deliverables, roles and responsibilities, and time frames.

Secondly, executive management must allocate the resources necessary to accomplish all of these required activities. This includes capital investments, personnel, facilities, and equipment. This goes back to the basics discussed previously in establishing the structure for the quality system. Executive management must make certain that the proper and adequate resources are in place to establish and maintain the structure, evaluation and alignment, automation, and continuous improvement of the quality system.

Management must ensure that the quality system is established and maintained in a manner that will collect and report adequate and appropriate data to management so that priorities and resource allocations can be effectively monitored and corrected where necessary.

Management must ensure that training requirements are established and that applicable training is provided. It must also establish the audit/assessment system. Remember, audits and assessments are the eyes and ears. Auditors should be some of your best people.

Executive management must demonstrate its understanding and use of the quality system as a strategic process if the system is ever going to be effective and successful. Most importantly, executive managers must *lead by example*. They must unquestionably be seen as the number one proponents of the implementation, maintenance, and continuous improvement efforts. One of the most effective ways, in my experience, to do this is *management by wandering around* (MBWA). I have used MBWA and found it to be a very valuable technique when used correctly and consistently.

MBWA is an involved, highly interactive, get-out-of-your office, executive management practice. It goes together well with an open-door policy. MBWA has made leadership more effective in many successful organizations. It helps senior management ferret out issues and allows time to chat with the people throughout the organization. It also builds communications networks and trust, if you follow through on what you discover.

At first, employees often suspect MBWA is just an excuse for management to spy and interfere unnecessarily. This usually dissipates when the walkabouts occur regularly, and if people start to see results from the visits.

MBWA can be particularly helpful in times of organizational stress: during and after a significant corporate reorganization, a workforce reduction, or a major product introduction or problem. If, however, you start MBWA during these crises or stress times, you will only add to the stress. If you have been practicing MBWA before these happen, then it can be extremely useful during these times. Tom Peters, a guru on excellence, states that managing by wandering around is a basis of leadership and excellence and calls it the "technology of obvious."[1]

One company I worked with wanted better communication. I suggested MBWA, as I had used it previously. We set up scheduled 60-minute walkarounds on both shifts every week. We published a schedule in the beginning so people would know management was coming. Management communicated what it was doing and why it was doing it. Amazingly, all of the executives cleared their schedules for these walks. After two or three weeks, people lost their suspicions and really started to open up. Management fed the issues into the CAPA system and tracked and communicated the results. Issues as minor as not enough lab glassware were resolved, and people started looking forward to the visits.

Management found out "more about their business in a matter of a couple of months than they had learned in five years." It has now been several years and the MBWA visits still occur every week. Management has added a semiannual activity where it recognizes contributors at a breakfast, lunch, or dinner (depending on the shift), which is prepared and served by managers. The people at this company don't just talk with management; they communicate.

At any company, executive management needs to get the quality system implemented, maintained, and improved. To accomplish this, executive managers must balance task versus people; because systems are where the problems lie and people are the most important resource.

To recognize this most important resource, it is important for executive management to celebrate successes. Initially, these may be small successes that get the process going; as the organization grows and matures, these may be scheduled celebrations as well. Do not overlook the importance and impact of celebration. Scheduled celebrations (quarterly, semiannual, or annual events) and nonscheduled rewards for specific achievements make people feel like they add value.

FUNCTIONAL/DEPARTMENTAL MANAGEMENT

Functional/departmental management heads up the day-to-day operations throughout the organization. Larger organizations may actually have two levels of functional/departmental management: one at the strategic level and one at the tactical level.

Whatever the structure and responsibilities are, there must be clear communication within and between functional/departmental management and executive management. Functional/departmental management must work with executive management to translate the strategic quality plans, goals, and objectives into specific metrics and tactical activities and deliverables that will ensure that those plans, goals, and objectives are met.

Functional/departmental management is the first line of defense for the quality system. Functional/departmental management works closely with the management representative to collect, collate, report, and analyze quality data and information. They act as the triage unit for issues, nonconformances, and deviations.

The organization's functional/departmental management must be vigilant and proactive; it must seek out information regarding events (deviations and nonconformances) and trends and work with the quality functions and management representative to create and maintain closed-loop feedback systems.

Because functional/departmental managers are the interface between executive management and the working population in the organization, they must be able to translate management goals, objectives, and information into terminology that the people in the organization can understand and apply. They must also be able to work with their subordinates and peers to translate daily data and information into management language of risk and costs. This is highly important, because if this does not happen, executive management will not have the proper information on which to base the priority and resource allocation decisions.

Functional/departmental management is responsible for ensuring that the procedures, work instructions, records, and forms are adequate and appropriate, followed and documented, and that changes and improvements to these are reviewed and approved prior to implementation of the changes and improvements. Functional/departmental management often does more wandering around out of necessity, but they also should practice MBWA on a regular and consistent basis.

THE MANAGEMENT REPRESENTATIVE

The management representative has an extremely important set of responsibilities. As discussed in the structure section, this person must be the caretaker (the ombudsperson and ambassador) of the quality system.

The management representative should not have any other responsibilities. Overseeing the quality system data and information and analyzing it is a full-time job, regardless of the size of your organization. In a very large organization, the management representative may also utilize the quality assurance and quality control resources to assist in these activities. This requires someone who has extensive knowledge of all of the quality system elements, quality tools, techniques, and automation and who can bring all of these together to ensure that the quality system is working effectively. The management representative must also have an in-depth working knowledge of all applicable regulatory, association, and industry standards and regulations that apply.

The management representative has the responsibility to communicate the status of the quality system to both executive and functional/departmental management. The management representative is also the conduit for information to and from the functional areas and departments. Accordingly, they must also be able to work with functional/departmental management and the quality functions to translate daily data and information into management language of risk and costs.

The management representative must evaluate and analyze the audit/assessment and CAPA information to monitor and report the real-time quality system status. This goes beyond just looking at the specific data; it includes being the Sherlock Holmes of the organization. This means that the management representative is constantly on the search for both the hidden trends as well as the obvious ones. This is why the management representative must have an in-depth knowledge and ability in a variety of quality tools, techniques, and, where applicable, automation.

Lastly, the management representative is not an honorary position, nor is it a position that is automatically assigned to the QA manager or director. This assignment must be well thought-out by executive management, as this position is an integral part of the structural foundation in terms of getting the right personnel. This person must have the ability to access and influence executive management, as well as functional/departmental management.

The management representative has connections to all of the functional groups and the CAPA system. Figure 6.1 shows the major connections that absolutely must be in place in regard to connecting the management representative to the quality system. To do the quality system justice, connection lines must be drawn from every circle to every other circle to ensure closed-loop feedback systems. It is the management representative's responsibility, working with the rest of the organization, to ensure that these loops are in place and functioning effectively.

Figure 6.2 is a representation of the connections within the entire quality system and shows the integration of the management representative. Notice that the management representative and the QA

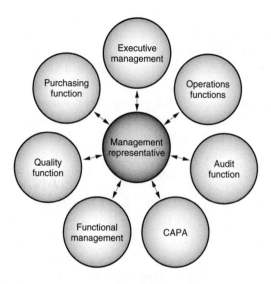

Figure 6.1 Management representative connections.

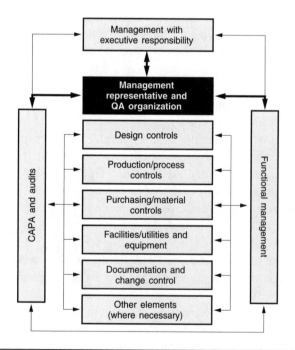

Figure 6.2 Quality system connections.

organization have been included together. This may or may not be the case, based on the size and structure of the organization.

Figure 6.2 shows the connections between all of the elements of the quality system. When going through the four phases as described in Chapter 4, make certain that you take this into consideration as you develop the architecture, connections, and linkages within and between quality system elements.

QUALITY ASSURANCE AND QUALITY CONTROL

There is sometimes some confusion between these two responsibilities. Figure 6.3 shows the relationship between the quality system and quality assurance and quality control. As demonstrated in the figure, quality assurance (QA) activities and responsibilities cover virtually all of the quality system in one fashion or another. Quality control (QC) is a subset of the QA activities.

There are items/elements within the quality system that are not directly part of the quality functions, but the quality functions perform many functions and oversee and monitor the quality data and information from all elements of the quality system, in conjunction with the management representative. The major items in the quality

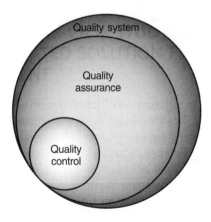

Figure 6.3 Quality system, quality assurance, and quality control relationships.

system that may not be specifically covered by the QA/QC activities and responsibilities include, but are not limited to:

- The administrative aspects of documentation, although some organizations have this under the control of QA.

- The administrative aspects of purchasing and supplier management. QA works with purchasing to qualify and monitor suppliers.

- Management reviews, quality planning, and setting of quality goals and objectives. QA is integral in translating quality goals and objectives into specific metrics and analyzing quality data and information.

- The administrative aspects of quality audits, although again, in many organizations, this is a QA function, while in others, it is a separate function. In either case, QA is involved in analyzing the results of the audits.

- Manufacturing (assembly and rework, packaging, labeling, storage, handling, identification and traceability, acceptance status, and distribution) activities. QA and QC have involvement here. See the upcoming sections on QA and QC specifically.

- Servicing, refurbishing, repair, and remanufacturing.

Quality assurance, as depicted in Figure 6.3, is a broad group of activities and requires resources with both a breadth and depth of working knowledge in terms of quality tools and techniques. It also requires breadth and depth in terms of product, process, and quality system knowledge. These people know what statistical and improvement tools to use and when and how to use them. They need to be adept at trend, risk, and root cause analyses, verification, and both design and process validation. The QA resources must have not only the knowledge, but also the experience and proven ability to apply that knowledge to establish, maintain, and continuously improve the quality system.

The QA function is involved in a much wider variety of activities and responsibilities, which include, but are not limited to:

- Process validation for all applicable assembly processes, facilities and equipment, in-process, analytical and laboratory test methods, sterilization, lyophilization, aseptic filling, packaging and labeling, water systems, electrostatic discharge, radio frequency interference, cleaning, environmental monitoring, and controlled environment, including process capability, installation, operation qualifications, master validation plans, process mapping, and flowcharting

- Statistical process control, process monitoring, and, where applicable, parametric release

- In-process, finished product, returned product, retention sample, reworked product, analytical, functional, performance, and laboratory testing

- Production, packaging, labeling, distribution, service and maintenance, rework and refurbishing, returned products, complaint records, and data review and approval

- Internal and supplier evaluation and auditing

- Sampling plans for acceptance, verification, and validation activities

- Design verification testing (for example, design of experiments, full and fraction factorials, Weibull testing, analysis of variance, response surface mapping, specification setting activities) and data analyses

- Design validation testing and data analyses

- Trend analyses (for example, regression analyses, comparative, and analytical statistical analyses) for complaint, CAPA, and audit data

- Risk analyses and risk management (for example, fault tree analyses, failure mode and effects analyses, failure mode and effects criticality analyses, hazard analyses, hazard analysis and critical control points [HACCP], and risk/benefit analyses)

- Root cause analyses (for example, fishbone diagrams, Pareto analyses, five whys)

- Continuous improvement activities (for example, balanced scorecards, Six Sigma, lean manufacturing, total quality management, just-in-time manufacturing, Malcolm Baldridge Award criteria, and cost of quality)

QA personnel must be able to effectively and efficiently analyze, evaluate, and reengineer processes. This includes establishing the performance metrics and monitoring. There are potentially many more activities and responsibilities that fall under QA, which are too numerous to include here. Suffice it to say that QA is a key brick in the structural foundation of any organization. It is mandatory that QA works closely with the management representative to establish and maintain channels of communication and information flow with all functional areas as illustrated in Figures 6.2 and 6.3.

QA personnel are generally more highly educated, trained, and skilled than QC personnel. Most organizations have engineers (mechanical, electrical, chemical, and biomedical), chemists, scientists, nurses, pharmacists, medical technologists, and other professional personnel with degrees as part of the staff. There may also be statisticians and biostatisticians on the staff.

In addition to their technical and scientific education, training, and experience, QA personnel must have a wide variety of quality tool, technique, and automation experience and knowledge. The QA staff must have the ability to apply a wide range of tools and concepts in reactive, proactive, and concurrent modes.

QA personnel are required to have diverse and extensive knowledge of the products and processes used not only in manufacturing, but throughout the quality system. QA activities are highly articulated with the CAPA, audit, change control, complaint handling, supplier management, and design control activities and deliverables. Organizations must see documentation as a required part of any activities they perform.

When interviewing potential candidates for QA functions, I always talk about investing hundreds of thousands of dollars, if not more, in them and their future. How are they going to provide a return on that investment? It is interesting to see how often even QA candidates have not thought about this. Hire the ones who have thought about it and can articulate how they would go about gaining returns on the investment that could potentially pay their salaries, or, even better, more than that amount.

The QC function is generally a subset of the QA function and is concerned primarily with acceptance activities and acceptance status. These include:

- Incoming inspection and testing.

- In-process inspection and testing, although laboratory testing is generally a QA function.

- Finished goods inspection and testing. Again, laboratory testing is generally a QA function.

- Inspection and verification of distribution orders.

QC may also be involved with manufacturing, packaging, and labeling line-clearance activities. QC personnel must be skilled and knowledgeable inspectors and technicians. They must be meticulous record keepers and reviewers.

World-class organizations have much of the in-process and finished product inspection done as part of a self-inspection process where each individual is responsible for his or her own inspection, rather than having a separate group of inspectors. This requires additional skills and knowledge, but can provide valuable benefits and actually lower resource requirements. That is because in many instances, a separate QC inspection group may be redundant and, therefore, not always value-added. This does not mean that you should lay off all of your QC inspectors. World-class organizations utilize previous QC inspector personnel to fill openings in manufacturing, calibration, and QA.

PURCHASING AND MATERIALS

Most organizations, based on my experience, are lacking in this area. There is adequate purchase order processing—materials are received, inspected, and put into the warehouse effectively—but purchasing data and supplier management are not top-notch.

In many companies, purchasing data refers to just keeping track of the purchase orders and tracking how long it takes to get things in and purchase price variances. What should happen is, purchasing data are gathered and used to proactively analyze the purchasing function in relationship to the suppliers. This requires that purchasing personnel be able to track, trend, and report specific data regarding things such as: incoming quality levels; outgoing quality levels; on-time deliveries; errors related to shipping, receiving, raw materials, components and products; and return-to-vendor issues. It is not enough to just track this information. Purchasing personnel must have the ability to analyze and utilize the information in order to make changes and improvements.

For example, ACME manufacturing is one of your suppliers, and you have a standing purchase order for 10,000 widgets to be delivered to your factory every Monday by 8 AM. Every couple of weeks, ACME thinks they will help you out and actually have them at your loading dock Friday afternoon. Is this acceptable? Maybe, maybe not. What if you do not have warehouse capability to store the widgets because you use dock-to-stock inventory? What if you do not have staff to unload them Friday afternoons because you work four 10-hour days? What if widgets require special storage conditions (for example, refrigeration) that is not available until Monday?

Purchasing personnel must know all of this and be able to relay the requirements to the supplier. Early shipments are not acceptable and, therefore, not an option.

Similarly, it is not enough to have an approved supplier list and to conduct supplier evaluations that are superficial. A true supplier management program is required. This means that the purchasing personnel must go beyond purchasing and material ordering and procurement to a truly proactive approach to supplier management (selection, evaluation, qualification, and monitoring). Purchasing personnel must have a basic level of technical understanding of the raw materials, components, products, or services they are purchasing. How can someone order chemicals, resins, electronics, or mechanical raw materials and components if they have no concept of how to interpret the specifications and requirements?

I am not advocating having engineers and scientists as purchasing agents. However, the purchasing agents should be able to conduct basic communications about the specifications without needing an engineer or scientist to interpret.

A few companies with whom I have worked have what they call commodity teams. These teams are broken down by the raw materials and components they purchase. The people on the electronics team know the basics about resistors, capacitors, diodes, integrated circuits, and printed circuit boards. In this way, they can communicate with the suppliers on basic requirements and basic clarifications. Certainly, there are times when the engineers must become involved, but this is the exception, not the rule.

The purchasing function should coordinate all of the supplier management activities including:

- Supplier selection, evaluation, and coordinating audits

- Supplier performance metrics and monitoring

- Supplier-related CAPA (corrective, preventive, and continuous improvement) activities

Many successful companies actually bring the suppliers into the facility and explain the products, the customers, and the impact of the supplier's raw materials and components on these.

All this means that purchasing personnel must work closely with the QA staff. Purchasing should gather and generate all of the data and information regarding suppliers—all of the associated purchasing data. This requires knowledge and skills in supplier auditing, tracking and trending of data, automated data gathering, and data analysis.

Material handling personnel are included here. They must have extensive knowledge of warehousing, storage, identification, traceability, handling, stock rotation and inventory management (first in, first out), and control processes (inventory turns, inventory costs, inventory accuracy, and auditing).

DESIGN AND DEVELOPMENT

Design and development personnel must have, in addition to the technical and scientific knowledge and skills, some very specific skills relating to design controls. These skills include the ability to gather and translate customers' (patients, users, and purchasing agents) requirements into specifications and actual products and processes in order to make the products. Purchasing agents are included as customers here because they are often the decision makers, especially if you are dealing with hospitals, HMOs, or governmental agencies. If you deal with purchasing agents, include their requirements as well.

Design and development personnel must also have the ability to develop, conduct, and analyze testing for both verification (the testing that shows that the products were made correctly and according to specifications and procedures) and validation (the testing that shows that the correct products were made according to customer requirements).

What's more, they need a keen understanding of risk analyses, including human factors.

OTHER FUNCTIONS

The other functions within the quality system, as described in Figures 6.1 and 6.2 (in other words, change management and documentation, production and process control, facilities, utilities, and equipment) all require a basic knowledge level and set of skills that are actually necessary to anyone who works within an organization utilizing a strategic quality system. The body of knowledge and skills, in addition to the required administrative, technical, or other skills that are job related, needs to include the essentials of:

- Basic risk analysis

- Basic root cause analysis

- Good documentation practices (attention to detail)

- Basic tracking, trending, and reporting of data

- Use of the CAPA system

- Basic quality system requirements (introduction to all elements and specific knowledge of portions that apply directly to their functions)

- Experience working in a regulatory environment (for example, FDA and ISO requirements and regulations)

- Product and service orientation

- Basic continuous improvement tools and techniques that are used by the company

---

Key Takeaways

- Understand the resources you need.

- Determine if the core competencies can be outsourced.

- Get the right people, train them, and retain them.

ENDNOTE

1. Thomas J. Peters and Robert H. Waterman, *In Search of Excellence: Lessons from America's Best-Run Companies* (New York: HarperBusiness, 2004).

7

The Role of
the Consultant

Are consultants necessary? Seeing as this book is written by a consultant, the obvious answer is yes. The question must be asked, however, "Are external consultants necessary?" Surprising to many people, the answer is, "Not always."

I have included a separate chapter on consultants because experience has shown that having an independent set of eyes and ears can be highly valuable and beneficial. I have found this to be true when I worked in industry as well as today. When I was in industry, there were always people in the organization that could be and were used as consultants, even though that was not their title. I found them extremely useful in helping to identify problems, evaluate situations, and develop potential solutions.

Whether you use an internal consultant or bring in an external one, there are some universal truths to consider. As stated earlier, the foremost responsibility of a consultant is to be a good listener. This is all about you, not the consultant. Well, actually it *is* about the consultant: can he or she be the resource you need? But a consultant's work is all about understanding and meeting *your* needs. Quality system consultants should work for executive management, since they are the decision makers. Remember, the role of executive management is to set priorities and allocate resources. Well, consultants are resources. Unless and until a consultant is legitimized by executive management, you might as well have the cleaning crew or night watch consulting. They will not be successful without management validation and support.

Anyone you use as a consultant must be extremely knowledgeable in the areas you where you need assistance. This seems self-evident, but there are generalists who may not have the breadth or depth of knowledge and skills to do you any substantial good. The return is not there so, therefore, do not make the investment! Quiz and challenge potential consultants, make them prove their worth before you engage their services. Ask them specifically about the return on the investment you are going to make. Even internal consultants cost money. There are usually charge-backs, cross-charges, or other stealthy ways of getting something from you in return.

Consultants must be independent. This does not necessarily mean independent of the company. It means independent in terms of being removed from the area, function, or project for which they are being asked to consult on. If the only way to get this true independence is outside the company, then that is where you should go. Independent consultants, when selected properly, do not bring the baggage and bias that personnel who are too close to the business, product, or process often have.

One of the most important skills a consultant needs is listening. Listening to you, the customer, about your needs, requirements, and expectations. Independent consultants must also have the knowledge, expertise, experience, and wisdom to know what to say, how to say it, and, often most importantly, when to deliver the message.

Independent consultants can actually save significant time and money. I have experienced many instances where I come into an organization and start looking, listening, and learning about the issues, products, and culture only to find that personnel are just getting frustrated. I find that they are looking for the wrong things or the wrong way. I use the analogy that the personnel are in a pine forest . . . looking for acorns. What's more, they cannot fully understand why they are not finding any. They are expending significant time, effort, resources, and money on a project that will never yield anything but failure and cost.

Independent consultants add particular value in that good, reputable consultants can add insight and solutions that your organization may not have thought of. Knowledgeable consultants can bring perspectives from other companies, other products, other functions and departments, or even other industries.

The role of a true consultant, internal or external, is to bring an independent set of highly skilled and knowledgeable eyes and ears to bear on the quality system and/or problems. This includes analyzing and evaluating against the four phases of the quality system.

RUN, DON'T WALK

If a consultant comes in and starts telling you right away what he or she can do for you, find an excuse to cut the meeting short and run for the nearest exit. A consultant should always start by determining what your needs and requirements are and then explain to you how their experience, expertise, and knowledge can help fill your needs and requirements.

You certainly will want to know and verify credentials. Examine their curriculum vitae and call some people with whom they have worked. Ask around, maybe someone knows or knows of them.

A good consultant should be able to talk with you to determine if there are any additional needs that you may not be aware of without proselytizing. You do not want to be preached to, you want a partner who can empathize and sympathize. This empathy and sympathy, however, does not mean that the consultant is your yes-man. A consultant should help you take an honest and holistic look at your organization, quality system, and particular circumstances, whatever they might be.

Good consultants come prepared. They have done some research on your company, have visited your Web site, have some basic knowledge of your products, and perhaps have more specific knowledge of the technologies your products use. You should do some homework as well.

You must be prepared for the more than likely possibility that you will get information that does not paint your company in the best light. If things were perfect, you wouldn't be using a consultant. So be prepared, do not get defensive, and don't take it personally. The consultant really is there to help.

It does absolutely no good for you to have a consultant who is not tough, thorough, and demanding. This does not require the consultant to be mean or gruff, just fair, factual, forthright, and, above all, courteous and respectful of you and your organization. This, in turn, requires the same from you and your organization. This gets back to legitimizing the consultant; if the people in the organization do not see the value-added perspective (which needs to be clearly communicated to the entire organization by management), they will not cooperate.

Consultants should not be looking to get you on the hook or milk you for all you have. The goal should be to establish a working relationship based on trust and respect. This relationship means establishing clear, concise, and unambiguous activities, responsibilities, deliverables, and time frames that can be put into a contract and costed.

You should develop a specific plan or statement of work that details exactly what you want from the consultant, how long it will take, and how much it will cost. Even internal consultants should be able to provide this information. External consultants should be able to give you:

- A solid plan

- Specific activities and deliverables

- Schedules, timelines, and milestones

- Cost estimates (travel expenses plus actual consulting fees)

- Expected returns (cycle time reductions, throughput improvements, reduced costs due to noncompliances, deviations and other problems, and reduced business and regulatory exposure and risk)

You can also ask to have a fixed price rather than billing by the hour or day. A word of caution here: If external consultants quote you a number of hours for a given price, then bill a lot of hours and give you some procedures, flowcharts, and templates that have not been specifically tailored to your systems and products, you should question this. Are you getting what you paid for?

Whatever the outcome of these negotiations, hold the consultant accountable. If things are not done on time and to the agreed upon requirements, then there should be some kind of penalty. This can range anywhere from a monetary penalty to having the consultant remediate any issues at no additional cost to you. Be flexible, but be firm. After all, you are investing in the consultant's services and you should demand an appropriate return.

If a consultant comes with some basic procedures, flowcharts, and templates that are generic, make certain that they are starting points and that the consultant will be charging you for customizing them to fit your needs, not for developing them. Generic procedures, flowcharts, and templates are often effective starting points because it is generally easier to edit than it is to create. Plus the consultant has the added experience with other solutions that may make a lot of sense to your situation.

Any consultant who comes to you with a packaged system that does not require customization to your needs and requirements should be avoided at all costs. A cost pile-up is what will happen. You will pay for the system and then pay for others to try and fix this system or end up paying for another system.

External consultants should be evaluated through the purchasing system for suppliers. Consultants are going to supply specific services and deliverables; find out if they can deliver. Select, evaluate, and qualify them just as you would a contract developer or manufacturer. It may take a little extra time, but it will be a good investment.

THE HEART OF THE MATTER

The consultant (internal or external) may play a variety of roles and perform several activities. The first is this: Get the strategic quality system in place, if there is not already one established. This can include establishing the basic infrastructure of the quality system. Going back to the computer analogy: A consultant can help you get the right computer and hook it up. Consultants can provide core competencies on an interim basis until the right personnel and resources can be identified and incorporated into your organization.

Consultants should also be able to teach and train your resources on regulations and regulatory requirements, quality tools and techniques, and continuous improvement.

If a quality system has been established, then their role is to assess and evaluate the quality system to ensure that it is strategic and that it has been translated into tactical, day-to-day applications that are effective and timely. If a strategic quality system has been established and appears to be effective (based on independent assessment and evaluation), then their role becomes one of assisting in automation and continuous improvement tools and techniques. A consultant should have a proven history of successful quality system planning, development, implementation, maintenance, and improvement.

Having consultants who have worked both sides of the fence and have been part of business—functional, executive management, and consultancy—brings some really valuable perspectives. I don't say this because that is my background, I say it because if your consultant has not been around the proverbial block a few times, you are going to be as much a source of learning for them as they are for you.

A consultant must understand the risk-based approach to quality systems as well as the regulations and requirements for the quality system. A consultant must understand and demonstrate an ability to identify and resolve business, safety, quality, and reliability risks as well as the regulatory risks. A consultant must also have the ability to match your needs with solutions that reduce those risks and add value to your quality system.

Consultants should *not* be viewed as the final implementers of your quality system. Consultants are there to ensure that the quality system is strategic, customer-based, will reduce risk, and be value-added. They are there to ensure that no major activities, deliverables, or responsibilities are missed. Your organization, however, must take ownership of the quality system and carry out the tactical activities.

Back to the computer analogy. It is your computer: you bought it and now you must use it. Consultants can assist with selection, installation, applications/programs, printers, scanners, hard drives, and RAM, and show you how to use them. But in the final analysis, the computer, and all of the attachments, accessories, and applications are yours to use or, in some cases, abuse.

With consultants, always think of where you are in terms of the maturity of your organization and the quality system. Get someone to perform activities and work with your staff to provide deliverables that are timely, effective, add value, and reduce risk.

Not all consultants are good consultants, and not all are bad. Equally important to recognize is that not all consultants can or should work on quality systems.

Executive management and the management representative should work closely with the quality system consultant to define the needs and the strategy. There needs to be frequent and regularly scheduled communication to ensure that the project is and stays on track.

Consultants must be able to function at two distinct levels. The first is being strategic with assessments and planning, and the second is being tactical: working with the functional/departmental management and staff personnel to get the day-to-day and practical activities and deliverables (processes, process maps, risk analyses, GAP analyses, procedures, work instructions, forms, training, and so on) accomplished.

To reiterate, a quality system consultant is useless—regardless of how good, reputable, and knowledgeable he or she is—unless and until executive management validates them and communicates and verifies the added value provided. This validation includes executive management providing the visible support and commitment to the consultant and the associated work.

Key Takeaways

- Know what to expect from consultants, establish your requirements and expectations.

- Get what you pay for.

- Good consultants (internal or external) can add significant value.

8

Business Models and Quality Systems

Every business evolves. All companies, even the multibillion dollar, multinational companies, started out as small companies at some point in time. It is important to understand where your company is and where you anticipate your company going. This is important because it will help establish not only the size, scope, and complexity of your quality system, but also the basic structure, connections, and timelines for the quality system.

THE BASIC MODELS

Companies generally fall into one of these basic groups:

- Start-ups
- Turnarounds
- Fast growth
- The silent majority
- Corporate giants
- World-class acts

Certainly there are other names for these groups, and some would argue that there are many more groups, but these are the basic groups that pooled experience has shown to be most evident. Each of these will be discussed in terms of how a strategic quality system is used in each of these scenarios.

START-UPS

Start-ups are generally smaller in size, which usually means limited capital, facilities, and resources. So does that mean that the quality system should be limited as well? Well, it depends on several factors.

It depends on executive management and the goals of the start-up. Remember, executive management sets the stage for the organizational structure, culture, and philosophy. If managers have a solid awareness, understanding, and commitment to a strategic quality system approach, then the battle is half won already. If they don't, a quality system to them is a moot argument. Establishing a strategic quality system, even if you only establish the structure portion, is a giant step in the right direction, and the cost is substantially less than doing it at a later date.

The first decision start-ups have to make, assuming they have some investment or venture capital, is the goal. Here the company determines which scenario it wants to follow:

1. Be a stand-alone company that will grow and prosper as its own entity.

2. Develop a technology (product or service) and sell it to a larger company, while you move on to subsequent technologies.

3. Develop a company that will eventually become part of a major competitor, either as an initial joint venture, association, or strategic alliance, or a straight merger/buy-out.

A strategic quality system approach can provide useful information here. It will help solidify the understanding that other companies with whom you might want to have partnerships or with whom you might want to merge or even sell your company to are, in fact, customers, and, therefore, have requirements that you must understand

and fulfill. It will also make you focus on risk/benefit analyses and decisions regarding your journey toward your goal.

In each case, however, the role of the quality system is slightly different. In the first scenario, in which the goal is to be a going concern independently, the quality system can be instrumental in developing your company and its products and services. This effort will require that capital and resources be set aside for the quality system. It is infinitely less expensive and easier to do this in the beginning while the company is small and then allow the quality system to grow and evolve with the organization.

If you have 18 people, maybe even fewer, it can be relatively easy and cost-effective to start your quality system. Start with a basic structure: The beginning is the right time to get this going. A strategic quality system will also help in setting business and regulatory goals and objectives. Remember that the quality system is customer-focused (both external and internal) and risk-based.

Utilizing a strategic quality system from the beginning will pay dividends in the long term. Many start-ups don't do any quality system work in the beginning because they feel that they cannot afford the time or money. They may not have an internal expert of quality systems. Staff are all involved in developing the new products that are going to revolutionize the current markets. If you do not take the opportunity to get a strategic quality system in place at this point in time, you have lost the first and best opportunity to do it. It will cost more in terms of time, money, and resources if you wait. And the longer you wait, the more it will cost. This is an excellent time to use an external consultant. You get help creating a functional quality system while receiving some training and developing a basic competency in this area. A consultant can also help you identify and understand the regulatory, association, and industry standards, regulations, and requirements that you might not even be aware of.

I know you are thinking, "How can a start-up company afford an external consultant?" It is a valid inquiry. I personally have spent time with small start-ups and can tell you that it was very value-added. I work mainly in FDA-regulated industries, so I will use an example from that arena. Let's say you and five of your university friends have a great idea for the next diagnostic imaging system. You know a couple of medical doctors who like your idea and have hooked you up with a venture capitalist who has agreed to fund two years of development. Your team gets a patent, develops an actual working prototype, and is ready to let the physicians try it. Now what happens? If you haven't thought about a quality system and started building one you have three basic options:

1. Hope a company is willing to buy your invention and can recreate the needed regulatory deliverables (design and development documentation, assembly, test and inspection criteria and procedures, development and submission of the required investigation device exemption and associated premarket notification or approval, and so on).

2. Partner with you to get all of this accomplished, although this will generally mean giving them something in return (a percentage of the company, sales and distribution rights, and so on).

3. Try to do this all on your own.

There are some very specific and rigorous regulations and requirements that have to be understood and met before you can even think about letting physicians try your product or commercializing your product. The list is too extensive to go into detail here. Suffice it to say that this is a good example of how a consultant can add real value, if you do not have these capabilities in-house.

If you did not do this proactively (and concurrently) with your product development, you may not even know what some of the requirements are, so how can you have expectations of satisfactory outcomes? It is definitely easier to do this proactively than it is to try and go back retrospectively and recreate the required documentation.

If you take the time, and it is not a lot of time, to get everyone on board and get the basics in place, you will have laid the structural foundation that can be easily built upon as the company grows. Think in terms of a house, a solid foundation is vital. Without it, the rest, now matter how elegant or strong, is in jeopardy.

If you plan to manufacture and/or distribute your products in the United States, the European Union, Japan, Canada, Australia, and a large portion of the rest of the world, then you must consider having a risk-based, strategic quality system in place. Regardless of where you actually manufacture and sell your products, this approach will still add value—to the company and the bottom line.

You need some expertise in these areas. *If you don't have it, get it.* I have worked with venture capitalists and investment bankers providing analysis and assistance regarding the state of small start-ups in terms of readiness for regulatory submissions and product commercialization. This approach will drive your organization to identify, understand, and meet customer requirements. This approach will also help you in the four phases—especially in the structure and connection phase.

Establishing the structure and connections is the important part to get accomplished early in the start-up scenario. The remaining three phases can be done as the company evolves and grows. There needs to be at least one resource that can dedicate time and effort to get the quality system established. This resource can focus on the quality system requirements, but the leaders of the start-up must understand and commit to the risk-based, strategic quality system and clearly communicate this to the entire organization if it is to succeed and become part of the organizational culture and basic business philosophy.

If you plan to sell your products or services to another company, or if you are looking to be acquired by a major player, then a strategic quality system increases the net value of your organization. Experience in performing due diligence shows that companies with a strategic quality system, even if it is in the rudimentary stages, get better deals in mergers and acquisitions. Major companies look at the quality system as a mandatory requirement. If it is not in place, they calculate the expected cost in terms of time, resources, and money and deduct that from the asking price.

TURNAROUNDS

Turnaround scenarios are becoming more and more apparent. These are the companies where the risks (business, regulatory, and quality/reliability) have gotten to a point where something has to be done. These companies can be divided into subgroups as well. The first being those companies that are being outcompeted and are losing margins, market shares, and profitability. The second is a subgroup often referred to as the *egregiously recidivist*. These are the companies that regulatory agencies have taken actions against through repeated warnings, legal actions, product seizures and impounds, and import embargoes. These companies are pouring millions upon millions of dollars into turnaround efforts. Two of the major root causes are a lack of a strategic quality system, or the lack of an effective quality system. In either scenario, the risk-based or strategic portions of the quality system are not in place or effective.

In these scenarios it is a delicate balancing act between just stopping everything and starting over and how much can be done while you try to stay in business. The option of shutting down is such a business risk that it is not usually a viable alternative. This means that it may take years and hundreds of thousands to millions of dollars to correct. This is in addition to any fines. The regulatory-based turnaround is more dire in that the time frame for reform may be shortened, and the resources to effect the required changes could be enormous.

To undertake any turnaround requires the most comprehensive, honest, and introspective analysis of the current situation and, basically, going through the four phases of the quality system from the beginning. This means, at a minimum, reevaluating the structure and connections and reviewing the evaluation and alignment of the quality system. These should result in a comprehensive, corrective, and preventive action plan that executive management can prioritize and resource adequately.

In some cases, this may mean that your company may have to stop doing certain activities and reallocate these resources to get the turnaround effected before restarting the curtailed activities. Companies have had to curtail or reduce development, quality, and manufacturing operations and reallocate these resources to the turnaround. Once the turnaround is gaining momentum and becoming effective, then the resources are reallocated to their original responsibilities.

The main thing to remember if you are in a turnaround scenario is that you have missed or disregarded customer requirements and are now paying the price. Had you invested in a truly strategic quality system, this would not have happened in the first place. Companies are spending incredible amounts of capital and resources to fix things when for a fraction of that amount, they could have invested in infrastructure and quality systems that would have proactively identified and remediated the problems.

I have worked with a company that had a series of recalls over several years. We calculated the average cost of a recall in terms of personnel time and product lost. Lost sales, lost customers, and other costs were not calculated and included. The average cost turned out to be $750,000 per recall. This was a fairly large-sized company. Some companies often spend significantly more per recall. Needless to say, the company had spent tens of millions of dollars on recall activities over the years. Management finally had an epiphany and realized it could no longer continue to do business this way; the regulatory and business risk were too high. It was also negatively affecting the company's stock price and market capitalization value. The company embarked on a path to reengineer the quality system. It spent over $5 million and nearly three years getting the turnaround done, but it has not had any major issues since then. This is still a good news/bad news scenario. The good news is that they turned it around, the bad news is that they waited so long. Had they invested half of the $5 million proactively, they could have prevented the recalls in the first place. Having an effective quality system years ago would have saved over $10 million. Figuring a $3 million investment, that still leaves a net gain of at least $7 million.

There are lists of excuses and platitudes that would fill an entire chapter in themselves. But they are all reduced in the final reckoning to rationalizations and lack of honest introspection. Companies either did not know or care about their customers, or they did not understand the true risks and consequences. Companies figured that one of two perceptions were correct: that things couldn't be that bad and secondly that they couldn't happen to them. *Both were incorrect.* They actually underestimated the risk and did not have an effective mechanism (a strategic quality system) in place to provide the holistic, introspective critique of the business's health. Strategic quality systems are designed to identify, remediate problems, and, most importantly, prevent things from getting this bad.

Strategic quality systems are insurance policies that reap huge dividends in cases like this. The cost avoidance alone is worth the investment, even if you don't get into the continuous improvement phase.

FAST-GROWTH

Fast-growth companies have two basic scenarios. The first is that your company is a start-up, which is taking off from the beginning. The second is that your company has hit the *mother lode*, and you are now faced with rapid growth.

In the first scenario, it is important to go back to the start-up section. Review it and get a strategic quality system established. Again, even if it is only a basic quality system, at least get the basic processes and architecture in place. Refinement, automation, and continuous improvement phases can follow later, but the basic architecture and infrastructure are critical elements for success. Regardless of what you might think, these are business essentials. This is where a consultant can prove to be very value-added. A good quality system consultant can help develop a quality system and provide training. He or she can also help evaluate and align the quality system, if you have one.

It is even more imperative that this happen in a rapid-growth situation. If you fail to get the quality system in place and functioning effectively, you are likely to find that your costs to put one in place later will have increased significantly. Also, the problems and issues that a quality system could have caught and fixed will be more frequent and more severe—the increased risk factors.

This second scenario demonstrates why it is important to think in terms of, can you afford not to utilize a strategic risk-based quality system? Many fast-growth companies put all of their capital and resources into the growth, not realizing that the quality system is, in fact, part of that growth. They fail to get the bigger picture: the quality system adds value in terms of reducing the costs, cycle times, and risks that the company faces every day. Always keep in mind that the quality system is the foundation of the business. It is not some ancillary bunch of procedures, documents, and records that you can get around to later or that really aren't that important.

Let us assume that you are in a fast-growth mode because you have discovered a great new product. Let us also assume that you already have a quality system in place. Does this mean that you can sit back and not do anything in regard to your quality system? Definitely not. You must utilize the quality system to plan, implement, and maintain the changes that will be needed with the increased capacity and output required for these new products.

Companies fail to recognize that the strategic quality system is a way of doing business. It is not there to make the organization look good or to satisfy regulatory requirements. If you think these are the reasons for a quality system, you are greatly mistaken. You must utilize your quality system to make decisions about where to go, how to get there, and how to monitor the business so that (1) you will know when you have achieved your goals, and (2) you will know how effective you have been in getting there.

The evaluation and alignment and continuous improvement phases play extremely important roles in this scenario. This will also point out why it is important to have a well-balanced quality system. Refer back to the quality quotient in Chapter 5. Make certain that your quality system has the capability and capacity for this growth. If not, take some time to make certain that you get it right. Part of the planning should include things like:

- Detailed risk/benefit analysis
- Contingency planning (what is plan B if plan A hits snags?)
- Updating the quality system as required
- Reestablishing quality goals and objectives
- Establishing new specific metrics to monitor progress
- Reestablishing priorities
- Reallocating resources (either the existing or expanding resources)

I am not advising stopping everything while you plan. But take some time to develop a plan that incorporates your strategy into successful tactics.

You should also be thinking about issues related to the rest of the quality system: design control for the new products, change management and design control if the change is to an existing product, regulatory submissions, impact on customer complaints and customer satisfaction, production and process control requirements, site selection and qualification, process validation and transfer issues, training, and new suppliers and their management, just to name a few. These principles apply to any fast-growth company regardless of whether your products or services are niche or mainstream products.

THE SILENT MAJORITY

This group represents the largest segment of companies. These are the companies that move along without major issues. In this segment, most companies have quality systems to varying degrees. Most are not truly strategically based, and many are in place because executive management sees the need for a quality system as a regulatory requirement. The organizations here are successful and profitable, although not as successful and as profitable as they could be with a comprehensive and strategic quality system.

While most of these companies do capture customer requirements when developing products and services, many still fail to base the strategic quality system on all of their customers' requirements. Most of the business practices are on the fringes or outside the quality system, and decisions are not routinely risk-based.

Elements such as quality planning, goals and objectives, specific metrics, management reviews, and a comprehensive CAPA system are not at the levels necessary for a truly effective quality system. The honest quality quotients for many companies in this condition are scores of 2, although some companies and certain elements may have scores of 3. This opens these companies up to regulatory risks and to business risks. Most of these companies are not as profitable as they could be if they had a strategic quality system, and many are not nearly as compliant as they could be or think they are.

Taking this a step further: this means that the business risks include issues such as increased rework and scrap, suboptimized margins, lack of capacity for manufacturing and distribution, increased systems downtime, increased customer complaints and decreased customer satisfaction (and subsequent sales and profit), increased lot/batch failures, and increased numbers of changes.

On the regulatory risk side (again I will use the FDA-regulated arena), this is often evidenced by: substantial FDA inspectional observations, warning letters and consent decrees or other actions, increased field corrective actions, and adverse events or medical device reports. While these items may not be independently catastrophic, their cumulative effects put a burden on the organization and point out quality system and architectural deficiencies. As stated previously, a comprehensive quality system would have identified and resolved these issues.

All of these issues lead directly to the bottom line of the financials. They are all symptomatic of an inadequate quality system (the quality system is inadequate or unbalanced in terms of quality quotient scores).

Not all of the companies in this segment are having these kinds of problems. Some are actually using a strategic quality system. Those that are utilizing this approach are successful and profitable. They generally tend to be small- to mid-cap-sized companies that have made the strategic investment in a comprehensive quality system. These are the companies with balanced quality quotients in the 3 to 4 range. They may have some elements that include some level 4 or even 5 requirements, but they are the solid state-of-the-art organizations.

This is a good place to be. In the professional sports analogy, you are playing in the big leagues and winning your share of games. From here you can determine if the leap to world-class is for you; it may not be. The investment and return on the investment may not be appropriate, and, therefore, the risk is not acceptable from a business perspective. Realize that going to world-class is perhaps the single most significant investment, commitment, and hard work–loaded endeavor a company can make.

These companies, however, represent the minority within this category. The largest portion of the companies in this category maintain their business using some of the elements and ideas, but do not fully apply or leverage the quality system. They may have some basic architecture, but they have not performed evaluations and alignments adequately. They may have architecture and evaluation and alignment, but they have not effectively automated processes to reduce costs and cycle times. They may have all of the first three phases, but they have failed to implement continuous improvement and are losing out on the quality system's full potential.

CORPORATE GIANTS

These are the large-cap companies—the big multinational corporations. Interestingly enough, they all have quality systems. These quality systems—even at these prestigious giants—are often not used strategically and are not balanced in terms of quality quotients.

This category faces the dilemma of centralized versus decentralized in terms of quality systems. Most have decentralized. There may be corporate policies and procedures, but most of the time, there are local or site quality systems.

The best solution, based on experience, appears to be a broad corporate umbrella of policies (and potentially a quality manual) that establish the basic what-to-do requirements. This may also include some high-level standardized how-to procedures for things like:

- Planning, setting goals and objectives, and management reviews

- Purchasing and supplier management

- Change management and document controls

- Distribution and servicing

A word of caution here: If you get too many or too detailed procedures at the corporate level, you are turning your facilities and sites into exact copies of each other. If this is not your aim, you will almost assuredly find that you have created problems for some of your facilities or sites.

The goal of corporate-level policies and procedures is to provide structure so that all facilities and sites meet the same requirements (what to do), but allow them flexibility in how to meet the requirements. A good quality system makes life simpler, not more complicated. This does not always translate into easier. Sometimes it will take work to get things running the way they should. In the long term, however, it must make things better. Otherwise, you have missed something in the development and implementation.

The corporate-level policies and procedures are then translated into more specific how-to procedures, work instructions, records, and forms at the local or site level. Many of the giants create their own problems in that they try to dictate highly prescriptive and detailed requirements that cannot be met at all of the local levels. This creates an environment of work-arounds. Local-level personnel are clever and bright. If something does not work, they will figure out a way to get it to work. Unfortunately, this, more often than not, leads to ineffectiveness or noncompliance to both business and regulatory requirements.

Some of these corporations actually have detailed procedures and work instructions at the corporate level. Experience has shown that this type of situation leads to problems, unless you are a McDonalds-type organization. I am not using McDonalds as a bad example. McDonalds is highly successful. I am using it to point out that if your facilities and sites are not all the same, then the highly detailed approach is probably not the best for you. Unless your corporation has the goal of making every facility exactly the same, in terms of structure (facilities, utilities, equipment, people, processes, products, work flow, and so on), then this approach is generally going to increase business and regulatory risk rather than reduce it.

If a strategic quality system approach was really in use, the corporation would gather input and requirements from the internal customers as well as the external customers. This almost always results in such a variety of requirements that only a broad policy can cover them all at the corporate level. The specifics of how to get this accomplished belong at the local level.

Corporate giants have a mix of scenarios. They can include all of the basic models within a single corporation and often do. That is why it is so important to have two levels of strategic quality systems for these types of organizations. The first is a corporate-level quality system that is 90 percent strategic: what-to-do requirements. This is accomplished with clear and concise policies and perhaps business-level processes. These processes are still at the what-to-do level, but may be up to 50 percent how-to. The how-to is mostly in terms of sequence of activities, not in terms of exactly how to perform specific tasks. For example, the quality system may require that there be a purchasing process. There could even be requirements indicating that a purchasing process needs to include the following activities, and even the order of these activities:

- Supplier management (selection, qualification, and monitoring)

- Placing orders (with approved suppliers)

- Receiving orders

- Verifying orders

- Monitoring purchasing data (and reporting it to CAPA and management)

If you are going to go to the process level, then there should be a process map depicting the basic sequence for each process. Notice, however, that there are no details concerning how to accomplish these activities, only the sequence. The corporate-level quality system establishes the basic customer-centric requirements that must be met.

The remaining 10 percent of corporate policies and procedures is tactical. It focuses on two basic areas: (1) what information is to be collected, collated, reported, and analyzed, and the corporate level's subsequent analysis of the information, and (2) how the corporate level will prioritize issues and activities and allocate resources (corporate-level management review and CAPA).

Procedures and work instructions include specifics regarding how to accomplish the activities and generate the deliverables. Procedures and work instructions also include specific roles and responsibilities.

The local-level procedures and work instructions will also have two components (strategic and tactical). The strategic portion focuses on translating the corporate requirements into local requirements, if this is needed. Often the corporate-level requirements are adequate; if not, then another level of detail is required at the local level. Local must work in conjunction with and complementary to corporate. There can be no conflicts.

Site-level strategic portions focus on the what-to-do at the local level, based on the corporate requirements (policies and, where appropriate, processes). Remember that all processes (procedures and work instructions) should have a flowchart/process map and a risk analysis. If you cannot flowchart or map a process, then you do not understand the process well enough. You should go back and get some of the internal customers who will own and use the process to help out.

At the local level, the vast majority of outputs are the tactical how-to procedures, work instructions, records, and forms. The more complex the procedure, the more in-depth the risk analysis. Utilize work instructions where procedures do not provide adequate detail.

Having local-level procedures and work instructions does not preclude the use of common procedures and work instructions. If multiple sites use the same systems and equipment, then perhaps common procedures are the answer. The decision regarding this is based on getting the internal customers who will use the systems, equipment, and procedures together and performing a risk/benefit-based analysis.

A common mistake at both the corporate and local levels is that the policies, processes, procedures, and work instructions are not written at consistent levels. This results in the level of detail varying within and between the procedures and work instructions. This leads to confusion and conflict, which in turn, lead to ineffectiveness and noncompliance.

Some corporate giants are utilizing the strategic quality system approach. Experience shows that there are not many giants that can state conclusively and honestly that the corporate and all local-level quality systems are at least state-of-the-art and balanced across the board; all of the quality systems meet at least the level 3 quality quotient criteria.

WORLD-CLASS ACTS

These are the companies that have gotten it right. There are not many companies in the category, and rightfully so. To fit into this category there are two basic criteria. The first is that the company fully embraces the strategic quality system and has successfully implemented all of the four phases. The second is that the company has come to the conclusion that state-of-the-art or best-in-class is not adequate and that they have the capability and drive to invest in systems that go beyond the norm.

These companies have completed integrated and holistic systems; they take long, hard, and honest looks at themselves and do not rationalize any data or information. All of the decisions are risk-based and include detailed analysis of the impact on customer satisfaction (both external and internal customers) with the external customer being the primary driver. These companies have specific mid- and long-term goals to reinvent themselves on a regular basis.

Executive management takes an active, participative role by utilizing: (1) management reviews; (2) quality planning, goals, and objectives; and (3) a comprehensive and holistic CAPA system. Executive management is accountable for and holds personnel accountable for the use, maintenance, and continuous improvement of the quality system. Executive and functional/departmental management spends time engaged in MBWA.

In addition to these traits, the organization is relentless in the application of value-adding automation and quality tools and techniques. It has a proven track record demonstrating excellence in reducing business and regulatory risks, reducing the cost of quality (both the price of conformance and the price of nonconformance components), and reducing cycle times for all business processes. More importantly, it has a proven history of consistently and continuously adding value to the customers.

For example, a real-life world-class company decided that it needed to add more value to its customers. Upon evaluation and investigation, it found that it and its competitors had raised product prices every year by an average of two to three percent. The company strategized on how to increase profits while not having a price increase for at least three years. The solution was to apply even more sophisticated tools and techniques to drive manufacturing costs down, maintaining prices to customers and actually increasing margins. The company decreased manufacturing costs an average of nearly six percent per year. The investment was just under two percent per year. The net margins increased by nearly four percent per year. The market share also increased by nearly seven percent because the company had created competitive advantage through the application of its strategic quality system.

I know that this seems like it is business savvy and not so much quality systems–driven. It actually is both, and that is a major point of this book. *The two are inseparable.* The goal is to create this type of synergy.

Not all world-class companies are large companies with enormous capital reserves. Companies do not need to be big to be good. They simply need to be good, *to be good.* This requires dedication, commitment, and communication levels not normally encountered. In these organizations, everyone knows the priorities, the application of these to their jobs, and exactly what the expectations are.

Management is strong, educated, and dedicated; and it knows enough to get the best people it can. Management in these companies sets the priorities and direction, allocates the resources, and then gets out of the way. Management manages the systems and directs the people. Issues are routinely solved at the lowest possible level and only the huge "showstoppers" that cannot be resolved at lower levels make it to management for decisions.

People in these organizations work and work hard—that is not to say that people in the other categories do not, but employees at world-class companies also work smarter. They work toward an uncompromising and customer-centric purpose. They do not come to others with problems unless they have already thought of at least one, if not more, solutions. Every activity is customer-centric and value-added. Those activities that are not are quickly and effectively identified and remedied.

People are regularly recognized and rewarded. The real focus of the quality system here is proactive identification of customer requirements and expectations (both spoken and unspoken) and effectively and efficiently exceeding those requirements and expectations. These companies never say, "Good enough." For them, every product is their best product, and every service is the best they can provide. There are no compromises, and there are no excuses.

In these companies, the quality system has been strategically established and is being strategically used. These companies have short-term (one year), intermediate (three to five year) and long-term (five to 10 year) quality plans, goals, and objectives, that are based on continuously and consistently increasing customer satisfaction (both external and internal) by identifying new and unspoken needs and/or exceeding their expectations by greater and greater margins.

A BRIEF EXPLANATION OF THE COST OF QUALITY

Best-in-class and world-class companies utilize the cost of quality as a major indicator/metric of their progress and value to customers.[1] (I have not specifically addressed best-in-class because they can exist in any of the models.) As discussed previously, the cost of quality is composed of two elements: what it costs to make the right products correctly (the price of conformance) and what it costs to do anything else (the price of nonconformance). The price of nonconformance includes making the wrong products or product mix and performing these functions either correctly or incorrectly.

Figure 8.1 shows three boxes. The first on the left is a typical cost of quality chart for a company that is not doing too well. The price of nonconformance (all but the upper left box) is elevated and represents a significantly larger portion of the total cost of quality than the price of conformance. The price of nonconformance can often be up to 50 percent of the annual operating budget.

The box in the middle shows what this looks like at best-in-class companies who have implemented continuous improvement through the use of a strategic quality system. The price of nonconformance and the total cost of quality have been significantly reduced, with the price of nonconformance well below 50 percent of the total cost of quality.

The box on the right depicts the efforts of world-class companies that now utilize advanced quality tools and techniques such as Six Sigma, Taguchi, and lean, to not only continue to lower the price of nonconformance, but also to drive down the price of conformance. This results in the highest possible quality at the lowest possible cost, which translates into maximum value to customers and shareholders.

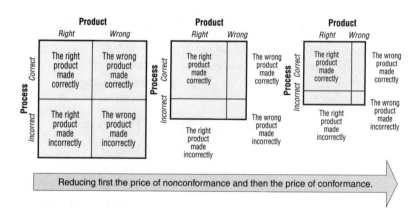

Figure 8.1   The cost of quality reductions.

THE CONSTANCY OF CHANGE

The one constant in business or quality systems is change. How companies identify, address, and embrace or confront change determines where they will ultimately end up. Think about your company and how it handles change. Do you react to events and changes or do you proactively seek out and leverage change?

Best-in-class and world-class companies do not sit around and wait for things to happen and change to occur. They proactively collect data and information to drive changes. They even go out of their way to figure out how to use the quality system to strategically create changes that will result in competitive advantage for their companies.

As stated at the beginning of this chapter, all companies evolve or at least change. Companies are continuously sliding up and down the scale, depending on a variety of circumstances. Companies can be hybrids of the models, containing aspects of several, and in some cases, all of the models. It is actually unusual to find a company that fits solely into one model. It is similarly unusual to find companies that stay in one model for extended periods of time, with the exception of the silent majority.

These explanations should demonstrate how a strategic quality system approach could help ensure that the movement is always in the right direction. They should also point out some of the strengths and weaknesses for the basic business models in terms of implementation and the use of a strategic quality system approach to business. Use these business models when you start establishing your quality system and the four phases. Also use it when you start doing your evaluation and alignment and when you calculate your quality quotient.

It is imperative to realize that all of the various elements and activities involved with establishing, maintaining, and improving your quality system are intertwined. No one part is more important, or less important. Some elements need to be done serially (structure and connections first) while the others (evaluation and alignment, automation, and continuous improvement) can often be done in parallel. Regardless, to optimize and maximize your quality system takes time, effort, and investment. It also takes serious dedication, education, and discipline.

Key Takeaways

- Know who you are as an organization.

- Know where you are as an organization.

- Know where you want to be.

- Be realistic in your evaluation, perception, and expectations.

ENDNOTE

1. Jack Campanella, *Principles of Quality Costs: Principles, Implementation, and Use,* 3rd ed. (Milwaukee: ASQ Quality Press, 1999).

9

Where Do You Go From Here?

To be effective, a company must have a quality system culture and an environment conducive to open communication and constructive criticism. The organization, from top to bottom, must embrace quality as a continuum from customers to products and services to relentless and constant improvement. Where you go from here is up to you. I have tried to provide not just the road map, but the direction and motivation to keep you on the right path and prevent you from going down the path of ruin.

YOU'VE GOT TO HAVE CULTURE

This has been stated before, but to start, you must embrace that a quality system culture is a way of doing business. It is first and foremost *customer-centric:* Every aspect of business is based on identifying and understanding customers and their requirements and then translating these into value-added products and services.

A quality system environment is not just an extension of the culture, it is the heart and soul of the culture. It incorporates business and regulatory needs as the warp and weft of the fabric of the business. It establishes an atmosphere in which each employee feels a responsibility to customers (both external and internal). People are accountable and expect everyone else to be accountable as well.

Good enough never is. The culture drives a proactive, rather than reactive, business model that continuously strives to seek out new ways to satisfy customers.

The choices your company has are relatively simple; the consequences are enormous. Is your goal to:

- Continue with the problems and issues, remain marginally effective and profitable?
- Be state-of-the-art?
- Be best-in-class?
- Be world-class?

It does not matter if your company is small cap, mid cap, or large cap; it also does not matter if your company has never had an eventful regulatory agency inspection or if you are under a consent decree. If you are in a competitive and regulated industry, the choices available basically come down to one of the following scenarios:

1. Your company can continue to do things the way that it has in the past and is doing now. If that includes the use of a strategic quality system, by all means, continue. This means that your balanced quality quotient is level 3 or higher, and you at least have some plans for automation, where appropriate, and continuous improvement.

2. If your company does not have a strategic quality system but has had success as a business and not had many problems with regulatory agencies, count your blessings. Your company has been extremely fortunate. Your company should undertake establishing a strategic quality system as soon as possible to reduce your risk, exposure, and costs. Review and utilize the four phases and the basic process to perform a gap analysis and then prepare an implementation plan. This may require some significant investments, but the return in the long run will be worth it.

Otherwise, the costs and risks in the long run will eventually catch up with you, and they can be staggering. Apply the "ounce of prevention is worth a pound of cure" concept. It is not a case of *if* you will incur problems, it is a case of *when* will they catch you and at what cost.

Your company could be risking its future. This scenario is what can lead companies into the death spiral: They get lulled into a false sense of regulatory and business security. We are making money, and we just cannot afford this right now, or the applicable regulatory agency was here last year and didn't give us a big list of observations or issues. When is a better time to get going? When you actually start losing market share, when your costs go up, or when a regulatory agency finally takes a serious look and does not like what it finds? It is always more cost- and risk-effective to be proactive.

3. If you have a quality system in place, but are still having business or regulatory issues, then you need to overhaul the quality system. These are indications that something is not working. This will most likely require redoing some of the system. To determine where to start, review the four phases and the basic process to perform a gap analysis and then prepare a remediation plan. Your issues are most likely to be in the structure or levels of your quality system. This means that the quality system is not balanced according to the quality quotient criteria. All of the elements within the quality system are not at the same level and this creates problems, especially with connections and interactions between the elements.

Go through the process map in Figure 9.1 and make certain that you haven't forgotten any of the activities. This is the same figure that is in Chapter 4; I have added it here so you do not have to thumb back to find it. This figure is important, as it should be the basis for designing and evolving or reengineering your quality system.

Correctly identify all of your customers and build your quality system around their requirements. If necessary, make a list of customers (both external and internal) and identify their requirements. Remember to include:

- Regulatory agencies, association requirements, and industry standards

- Business partners

- Third-party (contract developers, designers, manufacturers, sterilizers, distributors, service, and so on) providers

- Internal process owners and users

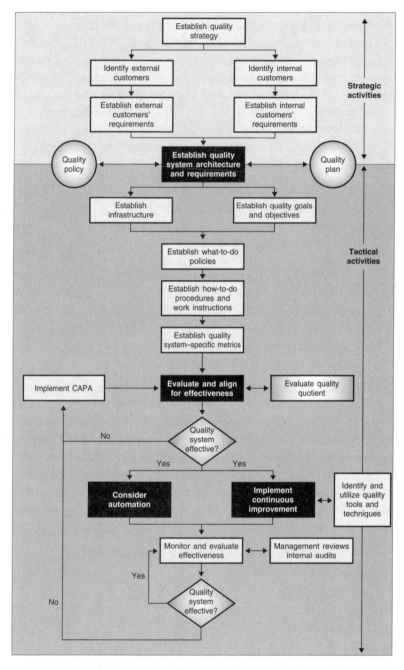

Figure 9.1 Establishing and maintaining a strategic quality system.

Reevaluate the quality system elements to ensure that all of these requirements have been adequately, completely, and clearly translated into specific activities and deliverables within the quality system. This must include assigning roles and responsibilities for these activities and deliverables as well. Ensure that these are then further translated into quality plans, goals and objectives, and specific metrics. Then reanalyze the results. This analysis must be open, honest, and comprehensive. It must be performed using a risk-based approach.

The first areas you should reevaluate are management responsibility and CAPA. Keep in mind all of the pieces by referring back to the chapter on quality system structure. Use the quality quotient process and evaluate your scores, focusing on all scores being 3 or above, and all of the scores being balanced. Use the information in Chapter 5 to remediate any discrepancies or gaps.

The single change that has the most impact is in executive management. Management doesn't often like to hear this, but take a look at the FDA warning letters, consent decrees, criminal and civil penalties. Who does this external customer (a regulatory agency) hold accountable? Similarly, if a company is not performing up to its fiduciary responsibilities, whom do the external stakeholders (Wall Street and the shareholders) hold accountable? The answer to both is executive management. Does this increase a company's business and regulatory risks?

From these statements one could surmise that changing executive management is the solution. This is not always the case. The real change is in getting executive management to read Chapter 3 on the basics of the approach and to realize that they have a responsibility to be knowledgeable in, committed to, and accountable for the quality system. The bottom line is worth repeating: the quality system must be a cultural paradigm that the entire organization not only buys into, but embraces and utilizes on a day-to-day basis.

Do not forget any of the management pieces. Management includes, at a minimum: quality planning, quality goals and objectives, establishing the structure and infrastructure, management reviews, appointing a management representative, internal audits, and training. All of these are focused on translating the customers' requirements into systems that meet (or where possible exceed) these requirements. The systems must also generate, collate, analyze, and report quality data and information back to executive management in order for them to make risk-based, knowledgeable decisions regarding priorities and resource allocations.

If all of this is in order, then the problem most likely lies with the CAPA system. It is actually difficult to imagine how all of the management pieces could be in place and still have major issues, but it sometimes happens. The CAPA system must be linked into every other part of the quality system. This means that there must be two-way conduits to and from CAPA and each element of the quality system. These conduits shuttle quality data and information to CAPA (and then on to management) and decisions (priorities and resources allocations) back to the departments and functions. Sometimes these connections are not adequately established or maintained.

When these two major pieces are established and effective, the rest of the quality system has to fall in line. This is the case because if these two elements are in place and working, then all of the other structures of the quality system must have been established, evaluated, and aligned correctly and effectively. As a result, your quality quotient should be 3 or higher.

If this is not the case, then the first steps toward establishing structure and connections have not been correct. These are indications that the process was not understood or established correctly. This usually indicates that customers or their requirements were missed, misunderstood, or disregarded; inadequate training (knowledge, awareness, and practical applications) has occurred; management is not being accountable or holding the organization accountable; or priorities and resource allocations were not adequate or clear.

The automation and continuous improvement aspects may not have been fully implemented, but the basic structure and connections should still provide an adequate base. The goal is that all aspects of the quality quotient must be at a level of 3 or better and must be balanced.

The final part of the process, once a quality quotient of at least 3 has been established, is to evaluate further progression. If the investments (capital, resources, automation, and facilities) required to move up to level 4 or 5 create a business or regulatory risk that is too great, stop. If this is a goal that makes sense (from a risk/benefit analysis perspective), then establish specific activities, deliverables, roles and responsibilities, and timelines for the progression.

The progression to levels 4 and 5, again, if warranted, can take several years. Therefore, put this into your one-to-three- and three-to-five-year plans. Set the priorities, allocate the resources, and start the journey.

Sophisticated quality tools and techniques will be required. Personnel with specialized and advanced skills, knowledge, and experience are vital for success. Utilize and apply the personnel, tools, techniques, and automation wisely. Develop contingency plans; monitor costs, budgets, and progress. Limit the number of projects and priorities to workloads that are attainable.

If you faithfully apply all of the concepts and principles detailed in this book, you should arrive at a point where your quality system is a competitive advantage and reduces your costs and cycle times, but more importantly, you will improve the value of your products and services to your customers, increasing their satisfaction. You will start to realize consistent and persistent improvements in both business and compliance performance.

If your company chooses not to invest in and utilize a strategic quality system, prepare for a rough and rocky road. From a business perspective, you will be passed and potentially even lapped by those of your competitors who implement quality systems. From a regulatory perspective, prepare to spend significant resources and capital reactively responding to regulatory agency issues. The word *spend* is used because there is no real return on these expenditures: the same problems will recur in different departments and functions, and with different products. They will not go away without a strategic quality system. You will pay over and over again.

Done correctly and comprehensively, a strategic quality system will become a way of doing business and can actually generate cost avoidances, cycle time savings, and resource savings that can be utilized to help fund some of the future investments in the quality system.

The Final Key Takeaways

- Identify and understand where your organization is.

- Realistically identify and understand where you want or need your organization to be.

- Establish goals and plans based on these.

- Execute the plan with discipline, direction, and dedication.

- Work hard, but, more importantly, work smart.

- Manage the system and direct people.

- Realize that sustained improvement requires continuous investment.

- Be accountable and hold others accountable.

- Include reward, recognition, and some fun.

Once you have accomplished all of this, do it all over again, and again, as necessary.

Glossary

architecture—The organizational infrastructure and additional resources required by an effective quality system.

awareness-based training—Training on the basic requirements and body of knowledge of a policy or procedure in accordance with local, state, and/or federal regulations; corporate or local policies; and standard operating procedures.

balanced scorecard—A strategic management system used to drive performance and accountability throughout the organization. The scorecard balances traditional performance measures with more forward-looking indicators in four key dimensions: financial, integration/operational excellence, employees, and customers.

best-in-class—Any notably successful member in an industry or industry segment that has implemented practices, programs, or policies that consistently perform at a level that meets all applicable accepted industry standards.

champion—Management leaders who ensure that resources are available for training and projects, and who are involved in project oversight reviews.

complaint—Any communication that alleges deficiencies related to identity, quality, durability, reliability, safety, effectiveness, or performance of a product after release to distribution.

compound aggregate growth rate (CAGR)—The year-over-year growth rate applied to an investment or other aspect of a firm using a base amount.

connection—A formal, documented link between two or more quality system policies, procedures, or work instructions.

correction—Action taken (repair, rework, adjustment) to eliminate the cause of a detected nonconformity.

corrective action—Action to eliminate the root cause of a detected nonconformity and to prevent recurrence.

cost of quality—The cost associated with the quality of a work product including the price of conformance and the price of nonconformance.

Cpk—Process capability index stated as the ratio between permissible deviation, measured from the mean value to the nearest specific limit of acceptability, and the actual one-sided $3 \times$ sigma spread of the process. As a formula, Cpk = either (USL − mean)/$(3 \times$ sigma) or (Mean − LSL)/$(3 \times$ sigma), whichever is the smaller.

customer-centric design—A process that integrates customers into the development of new products or changes to existing products.

design input—Intended users and user needs translated into physical, functional, and performance characteristics and/or requirements.

design output—The final product specifications resulting from development, including the actual product, master documentation, packaging, and labeling.

design verification—Confirmation by examination and provision of objective evidence that specific requirements (predetermined) have been fulfilled.

design validation—Establishing by objective evidence that product specifications conform to user needs and intended uses.

deviation—A departure of a quality characteristic from its intended level or state that occurs with severity sufficient to cause an associated product or service not to meet a specification requirement.

due diligence—The process by which inquiries are conducted for the purposes of timely, sufficient, and accurate disclosure of all material statements/information or documents that may influence the outcome of the transaction.

earnings before income taxes (EBIT)—Revenues less cost of goods sold and selling, general, and administrative expenses. In other words, operating and nonoperating profit before the deduction of interest and income taxes.

establish—Define, document, and effectively implement.

executive management—Senior employees who have the authority to establish or make changes to the quality policy and quality system.

failure mode and effects analysis (FMEA)—A disciplined bottom-up approach (procedure and tools) of risk analysis used to identify every possible failure mode of a process or product and then determine the frequency and impact of the failure to determine its effect on other sub-items and on the required function of the product or process. FMEA is also used to rank and prioritize the possible causes of failures as well as develop and implement preventive actions, with responsible persons assigned to carry out these actions.

fault tree analysis (FTA)—A disciplined top-down approach (procedure and tools) of risk analysis used to identify every possible undesirable event and the applicable failure mode of a process, product, or component.

field action—Any action taken to correct and/or prevent nonconformities once products have been released for distribution.

form—A document or template that contains required activities, signatures, and/or dates associated with specific procedures and/ or work instructions.

functional/departmental management—Senior employees who oversee the day-to-day operations throughout an organization.

Ishikawa (fishbone) diagram—A brainstorming technique used to facilitate root cause analysis.

just-in-time (JIT)—A planning system for manufacturing processes that optimizes availability of material inventories at the manufacturing site to only what, when, and how much is necessary.

kaizen—Japanese term that means continuous improvement.

knowledge-based training—Training to develop a practical application-level understanding and use of requirements of a policy, procedure, or work instruction in accordance with local, state, and/or federal regulations, corporate or local policies, and standard operating procedures.

lean—A process focused on the elimination of waste in every area of production including customer relations, product design, supplier networks, and factory management.

market capitalization—The total market value of a company, calculated as the current stock price times the number of shares outstanding. Small cap = stocks of companies with a market capitalization of less than $1 billion. Mid cap = stocks with a market capitalization of between $2 billion to $10 billion. Large cap = stocks of companies with a market capitalization of $5 billion or more.

metrics—Specific quantifiable data that are used to monitor and measure performance of a process, goal, or objective.

net present value—The present value of the expected future cash flows minus the cost.

nonconformance—A departure of a process from its intended level or state that results in failure to meet specified requirements.

nonconformity—A departure of a quality characteristic from its intended level or state that occurs with severity sufficient to cause an associated product or service not to meet a specification requirement.

objective evidence—Information that can be proven true, based on facts obtained through observation, measurement, test, or other means.

poka yoke—Japanese term that means mistake-proofing by preventing incorrect parts from being made or assembled, or quickly and easily identifying a flaw or error.

policy—A statement of intent, commitment, and/or requirements.

preventive action—Action taken to prevent the causes of a potential nonconformity or nonconformance or other undesirable situation in order to prevent occurrence.

price of conformance—An organization's investment in the quality of its products as a part of the cost of quality for a work product. Cost of conformance is the total cost of ensuring that a product is of good quality and includes costs of quality assurance activities such as standards, training, and processes, and costs of quality control activities such as reviews, audits, inspections, and testing.

price of nonconformance—The total cost to the organization of failure to achieve a good quality product. It includes both in-process costs generated by quality failures, particularly the cost of rework; and post-delivery costs, reperformance of lost work (for products used internally), possible loss of business, possible legal redress, and other potential costs.

procedure—An established series of activities, deliverables, and responsibilities that result in the completion of specified tasks.

process validation—Establishing objective evidence that a process consistently produces a product meeting its predetermined specifications.

quality objectives—Specific quantifiable goals strived for or aspired to.

record—A completed form or template that demonstrates that the activities and deliverables specified in a procedure or work instruction have been successfully completed.

return on investment (ROI)—Net realized value as a proportion or percentage of the initial investment.

risk analysis—A technique to identify and assess factors that may jeopardize the success of a project or achieving a goal, including defining preventive measures to reduce the probability of these factors from occurring and identifying countermeasures to successfully deal with these constraints when they develop.

risk management—The decision-making process (combination of three steps: risk evaluation, exposure and control, and monitoring) involving considerations of business, safety, economic, regulatory, scientific, and engineering factors with relevant risk assessments relating to a potential hazard so as to develop, analyze, and compare regulatory options and to select the optimal response for mitigating or eliminating the risk.

Six Sigma—A process designed to increase profits by eliminating variability, defects, and waste that undermine customer loyalty.

skill-based training—Training on the ability and/or competency to perform a procedure or task according to a defined level or standard and in accordance with local, state, and/or federal regulations, corporate or local standard operating procedures, or work instructions.

state-of-the-art—The level of development (as of a device, procedure, process, technique, or science) reached at any particular time as a result of the use of current modern methods.

subject matter expert (SME)—A person with a high degree of technical knowledge and skill in a given area of expertise.

trend—A series of data points, metrics, or measurements that indicate the general direction (positive or negative) of process, product, or system results.

work instruction—An established series of detailed steps and activities, deliverables, and responsibilities that result in the completion of specified tasks.

validation master plan (VMP)—A document that establishes the total definition of how the system will be designed and developed to fulfill the requirements specification including an overview of the entire validation operation (installation, operation, and performance qualifications) and its organizational structure, content, and planning. The core of the VMP is the list/inventory of the items to be validated and the planning schedule.

world-class—Any notably successful member of the set of organizations that has implemented practices, programs, or policies that consistently demonstrate performance at a level that exceeds applicable accepted industry standards.

work instruction—An established detailed sequence of steps, activities, deliverables, and responsibilities that must be completed and documented for specified tasks.

Index

A

accountability, 32, 45, 51–52
architecture and connections, building,
  40–74
assessments, 54–55
audit/assessment system, 117
audits, 54–55
automation, 22, 23, 79–83
  areas for implementation, 81–82
  caution, 79–80
  customization and implementation,
    81
  establishing requirements, 81
  understanding your goals for, 82

B

best-in-class, 2, 8
bonuses, 51–52
business analyses, 5
business models, basic, 141–57
  corporate giants, 152–55
  fast growth, 148–50
  silent majority, 150–51
  start-ups, 142–45
  turnarounds, 145–47
  world-class acts, 155–57
business practice effectiveness, 12
business risks, 36, 88. *See also*
  regulatory risks

C

calibration and maintenance, Q^2
  criteria, 107–8
centralized versus decentralized, 50
change, 159
change management, 12
change management and
  documentation
  architecture and connections,
    65–67
  Q^2 criteria, 98–99
commitment, 116
commodity teams, 129
communication, 31, 116
compensation, 51–52
competency, 32–33
competition, 2
conformance, price of, 158
consultants, 133–39
  accountability, 137
  external, 135–37, 143–44
  independent, 134–35
  roles and activities, 137–39
  skills, 134–35
continuous improvement, 59, 83–85
  investment, 84–85
  tools and techniques, 84
contracts, 72
corporate giants, 152–55
  levels of strategic quality systems,
    153–55

corporate-level quality system, 153–54
corrective actions, 58. *See also*
        corrective and preventive
        action (CAPA)
corrective and preventive action
        (CAPA), 12
    architecture and connections,
        57–61, 166
    examples, 61–62
    Q^2 criteria, 94–96
    system, 58–61
corrective and preventive action
        system, 58–61
    issues (events and trends), 59
    main goals, 58
    set up to handle three situations,
        60–61
cost curve, 10–11
cost of quality, 6–9, 157–58
Crosby, Philip, 7
cultural change, 28, 51–52
culture, 161–62
customer complaints, 58, 77
customer focused, 8
    design and development system,
        62–63
customer requirements, 30–31, 39,
        43, 62
customer satisfaction, 2, 31
    lack of, 1
    metrics, 52
customer-centric, 161
customers
    external, 42, 163
    internal, 39, 42, 163
    knowing and understanding, 2
    regulatory agencies as, 9, 24, 39
customers' needs, 42
cycle times, 31

D

delivery, on-time, 73
Deming, W. Edwards, 20
departmental management. *See*
        functional/departmental
        management
design and development personnel,
        129–30

design and development system,
        customer-focused, 62–63
design changes, 63
design control, 12–13
    architecture and connections, 62–64
    examples, 64–65
    Q^2 criteria, 96–97
design validation, 63
design verification, 63
design-transfer checklists, 63
discipline, 33–34
    lack of, 34
documentation
    and connections, 77
    design control, 63
documentation, change management
        and, 65–67
    review and approval, 66

E

employee problems, 45
evaluation of the quality system,
        74–79
    problems, 74
    simplified linkages, 75–76
evaluation tool, 5–6
executive management, 116–19
    basic functions, 117
    management by wandering around
        (MBWA), 118

F

facilities, equipment, and utilities, 42
    architecture and connections,
        70–71
    examples, 71
    special needs, 70
fast growth, 148–50
    planning, 149
    quality system, 148–50
field actions, costs associated with, 1–2
fishbone, 20
forms, 50
foundation, 11–16
functional/departmental management,
        119–20

G

gap analysis, 77
Global Harmonization Task Force
(GHTF), 21
goals, setting, 89–91

I

inefficiency, 51
information hoarding, 116
information technology, 22, 23–24
infrastructure, 40, 42
injunction, xv
inspection and testing, 71
  Q^2 criteria, 105–7
integrated quality system, 49–50
intellectual property, 4
interactive audits/assessments, 55
internal audit, Q^2 criteria, 99–100
International Conference on
Harmonization (ICH), 21–22

J

Juran, Joseph M., 20

L

lead by example, 117
line manager, 28
local-level quality system, 154–55

M

macromanaging, 43
Malcolm Baldrige National Quality
Award (MBNQA), 16
management, 14, 165–66
  accountability, 32, 45, 51
  architecture and connections,
    50–51
  audits, 54–55
  awareness and understanding,
    30–31
  discipline, 33–34

examples, 56–57
metrics, 52
objectives, 52–53
practices and systems, 43–47
problems, 53–54
as root cause of quality system
    problems, 45–47
strategic quality planning, 52
management by wandering around
    (MBWA), 118
management commitment and com-
    munication, 31
management direction, 32
management of the quality
    system, 33
management representative, 54,
    120–23
management responsibility, 12
  Q^2 criteria, 92–94
  in strategic quality system, 54
material handling personnel, 129
merit increases, 51–52
metrics, quality system effectiveness,
    51–52
micromanagement, 33
micromanaging, 43, 44
money, 14

N

nonconformance, price of, 158
nonconforming product, Q^2 criteria,
    108–10

O

on-time delivery, 73
organization infrastructure, 40
outsourcing, 115, 116

P

people and processes, 42
people problems, 53
perception, 4
personal gain, 116
personnel, 40, 41–42, 44

as root cause of quality system
problems, 53
workload, 52–53
personnel, educated and
knowledgeable, 30
CAPA system, 59
objectives, 32
planning, 51
policies and procedures, xix
prevention, 44
preventive actions, 58. *See also*
corrective and preventive
action (CAPA)
priorities, 32, 44, 54
prioritizing, 5–6
proactive, 50–51
proactive actions, 58
proactive approach, 9, 10, 15–16
proactive business model, 162
process validation, 63
processes and systems, 41
production and process control
architecture and connections,
68–69
examples, 69
Q^2 criteria, 102–4
standard inclusions, 68
progression planning, 47
projects, prioritizing, 5–6
purchasing and materials, 127–29
personnel, 128–29
Q^2 criteria, 104–5
purchasing and supplier
architecture and connections,
71–73
examples, 73–74

Q

quality
cost of, 6–9, 157–58
highest possible, 31
investment, 7, 14
quality assurance, 33
personnel, 126–27
quality assurance and quality control,
123–27
quality assurance function, 124–27
quality control function, 127

quality control personnel, 127
quality is free, 7
quality of management, 33
quality quotient (Q^2), evaluating,
89–113
criteria, 91–112
scorecard, 89–90
scores, 91–92, 112–13
setting goals, 89–91
understanding, 112–13
versus risk, 88
quality quotient (Q^2) criteria,
91–112
calibration and maintenance,
107–8
CAPA, 94–96
change management and
documentation, 98–99
control of nonconforming product,
108–10
design control, 96–97
inspection and testing, 105–7
internal audit, 99–100
management responsibility,
92–94
production and process control,
102–4
purchasing and material control,
104–5
servicing and installation,
110–11
statistical techniques, 111–12
training, 101–2
quality risks, 35–36
quality system
basic architecture, 48
customer-centric, 161
effective and efficient, 8
elements, 42–43
goals, 78–79
integrated, 49–50
investment, 14
phases, 39–85
reevaluating, 165
skills required, 115–31
value, 3–4
quality system, phases, 39–85
automating, 79–83
building the architecture and
connections, 40–74

continuous improvement, 83–85
  evaluating and aligning, 74–79
quality system culture, 161–62
quality system effectiveness metrics,
  51–52
quality systems
  evolution, 19–22
  problems, 53–54
  tools and techniques, 22–25

R

reactive, 50–51
reactive actions, 58
reactive approach, 9, 10,15
recall action, xv
recalls, 147
regulated industry, 3
regulations, 21, 24
regulatory agencies
  as customers, 9, 24, 39
  requirements, 15
regulatory inspections and findings,
  9–10
regulatory risks, 87–88, 90, 150–51
regulatory-related risks, 36
reliability risks, 35–36
requirements, 21, 24
resource allocation, 54
responsibility, 32
return on investment, 11, 14–15
revalidate, 70
risk, 87–88
  eliminating, 36
risk analysis, 35
risk management, 35, 36, 37
risk-based analysis, 35–37
risk-based approach, 24
risk/benefit analysis, 59–60
risks, identifying and quantifying, 5
root cause analysis, 20
  in CAPA system, 59

S

safety risks, 35
servicing and installation, Q^2 criteria,
  110–11

Shewhart, Walter A., 19–20
silent majority, 150–51
  business and regulatory risks,
    150–51
  quality system, 151
simplified linkages, 75–76
standards, 21
start-ups, 142–45
  goal, 142
  quality system, 142–45
state-of-the-art, 8, 155
statistical techniques, Q^2 criteria,
  111–12
strategic planning, 47–48
strategic quality system, effective
  establishing the basics, 28–34
  implementation, 28
  phases, 27
  risk-based analysis, 35–37
strategic quality systems, design, 147
subject matter experts (SMEs), 33
success, celebrate, 119
supplier management, 71–73
supplier management activities, 129
supplier performance, 72–73
suppliers, selecting, 72

T

technicians and assistants, 33
training, 47, 55
  Q^2 criteria, 101–2
turnarounds, 145–47
  quality system, 146–47
  subgroups, 145–46

V

validation master plan, 63

W

waste, 1
world-class acts, 155–57
  executive management, 156
  Q^2 criteria, 155
world-class capability, 8

7